VOICE-OVERS

D1489093

VOICE-OVERS

---

a practical guide

BERNARD GRAHAM SHAW

Routledge • New York

For Julia, Caroline, Susannah, Marianne, and David.

First published in North America in 2001 by
Routledge
29 West 35th Street
New York, NY 10001
www.routledge-ny.com
Routledge is an imprint of the Taylor & Francis Group
Originally published in 2000 by
A & C Black (Publishers) Limited
35 Bedford Row, London WC1R 4JH

ISBN 0-87830-115-1

Cataloguing-in-Publication data is available
from the Library of Congress

Cover photograph of Robbie Stevens recording TV links
for Channel 4.

Typeset in Sabon by
Florence Production Ltd, Stoodleigh, Devon

Printed and bound in Great Britain by
Creative Print and Design (Wales), Ebbw Vale

Contents

Acknowledgements

In writing this book I have become increasingly aware that it is the fusion of many influences and experiences.

I am pleased to acknowledge the very positive effect that the following people have had on my thinking: Paul Bura, Harriet Buchan, John Miles-Brown, Joseph Clarke of the Roy Hart Theatre, Gordon House, Martin Jarvis, Diana Wyn Jones, Miriam Margolyes, Spike Milligan, Patsy Rodenburg, Melinda Walker, Pam Wardell, and Fred Vohralík. To the many hundreds of 'voice-over' people who chose to put themselves in my hands I would say that I learnt as much from them as, I hope, they did from me.

My thanks also to the people who gave invaluable help in the many practical matters which surrounded the creation of this book and the accompanying CD: Jan Collins and Bobby Heath of Mood Spectrum Music Publishers; Robin Ochs, Chantal Cleven, and John McLeod, of or formerly of Vidox Video Productions; Mary Kalemkerian and Peter Donaldson at the BBC; Peter Gold at The Excellent Voice Company; Julia Vohralík for her most musical contributions to the CD; and Tesni Hollands at A & C Black for patiently guiding me through the unknown territory of writing a book.

I am very grateful to the following for giving me permission to use their scripts:

Bacardi-Martini Ltd for Bombay Sapphire, Bates UK for Safeways, Denis Bond and Scholastic Ltd for the extract from *The Dragon Who Couldn't Help Breathing Fire*, BT for BT Callminder, Crisis for Crisis at Christmas, Paul Bura for The Highwayman, Nell Dunn and Amber Lane Press for the extract from *Steaming* and Alan Brodie Representation Ltd 211 Piccadilly, London W1V 9LD for audio copyright from *Steaming*, Hoseasons Holidays Ltd for Hoseasons Holidays, Leeds Castle Foundation for Leeds Castle, The Rev. Christopher Mitchell for Intergalactic Federation, Nestlé UK for Black Magic and Black Gold, Procter & Gamble for Pantene Hairspray, Reader's Digest Association for Birds of the Seashore which is an edited extract from *Secrets of the Sea*, Sky Television for Sky Digital, R Twining & Co Ltd for English Breakfast Tea which is adapted from an advert originally produced by Saatchi and Saatchi Advertising, Viking Direct for The Pricebuster Sale, Vidox Video Productions for Quinta Da Rosa, Tanker Safety, and Thin Walled Tube.

All unattributed scripts are the copyright of the author and may be used in the production of voice tapes or as teaching material.

The original music on the CD was composed and performed by either Bernard Shaw or Bobby Heath, is published by Mood Spectrum Music Publishers, and the rights are administered by MCPS in London.

1

The World of Voice-overs

There is a well-known saying much beloved of men in bars and changing rooms: 'It isn't what you've got, it's what you do with it that counts!' Having a beautiful voice will not make you a successful voice-over artist any more than having long, slim fingers will make you a world-famous guitarist.

We went out for a meal last night. It was all most enjoyable, his mother came too. When we took her home I gave her a box of chocolates. 'Chocolates!' she said. 'It shows how much you care!'

A 'voice-over' is a person who can read this script and, by giving it two completely different interpretations, report on either the success or failure of the evening. Politicians refer to it as putting a 'spin' on something. Listen to the first two tracks on the CD and you will hear this script being performed in two entirely different and conflicting ways. In both cases the script is read accurately.

Success in voice-over is not a question of class or accent. It is a question of clarity of thought and diction coupled with the ability to communicate the subtle thoughts and desires normally masked by mere words.

There is an astonishing amount of work available for voice-over artists. Radio and TV commercials, CD roms, computer games, telephone information systems, recorded announcements, instructional videos and tapes, cartoons, talking books and documentary films all need voices.

Many years of research and vast sums of money have been spent on developing the 'perfect' speech synthesiser. Yet although it may be electronically 'measured' as being 99.9% accurate humans still hear speech synthesisers as being no better than a cheap child's toy. The brain/hearing combination in humans is astonishingly sensitive and is capable of understanding more than the superficial information conveyed by words. Unlike a machine, the human voice can both convey and detect attitude (mental and physical), as well as

1

mood and emotion. There is no acceptable substitute for a human voice, and with the proliferation of entertainment and communication media the need for real people with real voices continues to grow.

THE VOICE TAPE

As in all growth industries the sharks are beginning to circle. They sense easy prey and pose a real threat to those dipping a toe in the gentle waters of voice-over. The bait is called a voice tape. The voice tape (often wrongly referred to as a demo tape) is an essential tool for those preparing to seek voice work. Only the famous are invited to do voice-overs without first producing a tape.

The demo tape is a demonstration of what you could do if only you were given a chance; the voice tape contains examples of what you *do*. It needs to exude the authority and confidence that a demo tape lacks. It's a matter of attitude and packaging. You only get one chance to make a first impression – so make a good one.

For most people the production of a voice tape seems an almost insurmountable hurdle. How do you get the material, who records it, and who tells you what to do? You may see adverts along the lines of 'Voice-overs earn £200 per hour – let me record your tape and show you how to get into the lucrative world of voice-overs'. Beware! Listen for the sound of snapping jaws. Be equally sceptical if 'The country's leading voice-over' offers to take you under his or her wing. If they are indeed what they claim to be they would be far too busy to teach, and would not be prepared to sell their time at teaching rates when they could be voicing a commercial for ten times as much money. If you need training it is better to approach a director rather than a performer. There is a Chinese proverb which states that: 'The puppet does not necessarily know how the strings are pulled'. In the UK, none of the leading voice-over artists teach for money. Some may be very happy to help and advise newcomers, but they will probably do this without making any charge for their services.

There are very reputable companies who specialise in producing voice tapes and offer help, advice and lessons. But they do not use money as a bait to catch you. Good people in this field hardly need to advertise. Avoid anyone who tells you how fabulous your income will be – if only you'll give them a large sum of money first.

The money involved in voice-overs is a continuing source of fascination for outsiders. One hears fabulous and tall tales of either the sums earned or the fees that just escaped. The reality can be rather different!

VOICE-OVER AS A CAREER

Tomorrow sees the start of our new summer sale. We're cutting everything: there's 50 per cent off beds, 25 per cent off carpets, 30 per cent off curtains, and a whopping 60 per cent off discontinued kitchens. So, if it's super summer savers you want, slip into Sharpes – just off junction 10 of the M25. Sharpes, we're so keen, we'll cut anything.

This is a typical script for a furniture and furnishings store advert. It lasts 20 seconds and should be delivered in an energetic manner. It represents the everyday 'bread and butter' advertising work. It is badly written, too wordy and unimaginative.

If you, as a voice artist, were booked to go into a local radio station to record this 20-second wonder you might earn £9.00 ($15). In a larger radio station serving a city this could increase to £15.00 ($24). If the script were to be broadcast nationally you would earn about £400.00 ($650). If you did the same thing for an advertising agency with a representative of the agency present, you would receive the same level of fees but an additional £125.00 ($200) per hour whilst recording it. If it was used in a national television commercial you would earn £125 per hour plus a fee of £5,000.00 ($8,000). These figures are approximate but show the huge range of fees payable for doing exactly the same job in differing locations and for different mediums. The script and the difficulty of reading it well in 20 seconds do not change. It remains as 62 words which occupy 20 seconds and can earn you anything from £9.00 ($15) to £5,125.00 ($8,200)! Were you to be famous you would command a much higher fee, but you would be wise to save your voice-over virginity for a much more interesting and financially rewarding suitor.

It can be a mistake to assume that there is a career ladder in the voice-over world and that, if there is one, the place to start is on the lowest rung. Showbusiness has changed. There are no more apprenticeships – by the time you have served one, the world will have turned and whatever it was that made you an attractive proposition will be out of fashion. Unknowns come from nowhere, rule their particular part of the world for five minutes, and then at the age of 22 disappear back into the oblivion from whence they came. If you put yourself on the bottom rung of the voice-over ladder there is a danger that it will be seen as your rightful place in the scheme of things. Subsequent advancement may prove impossible as the higher rungs will be crowded with unknowns who flew in from nowhere. Being 'good' is not necessarily enough or even desirable. Being 'good at marketing' is what really counts! However, if you *are* good at doing

3

the job you stand a better chance of hanging on to your particular rung for a lot longer than most. Equally, you stand a much better chance of having a longer career if your voice is not a 'fashion statement'; fashions change but quality lasts for ever.

In theory, anyone can become a voice-over artist. The male voice-over cliché is the deep, silky voice selling an exotic fragrance. The female cliché is the sexy-voiced temptress consuming an ice-cream or chocolate bar. Clichés come into being because they work, but they are not the only options. In the voice-over world there are potential openings for all types of voices. Some are considered to be more commercial or more 'useful' than others and so will be given a disproportionate share of the work. Regional accents are no longer frowned upon – it is not necessary to speak perfect the RP (received pronunciation) which used to be known as 'Oxford English'. There is at least as much work for mature voices as for young, enthusiastic ones. There are more people in their 50s and 60s than there have ever been, and most of them want to deal with someone they consider to be of a similar age. A mature voice used to advertise a nursing home is likely to get a better response than the nasal tones of a 'bright young thing'.

It is popularly assumed that the route to success is in finding a voice agent then sitting back and waiting for both work and money to come rolling in. Yet most voice-overs are performed by specialists running their own one-man business. They may have an agent and a manager but they do not make the mistake of giving them power over their professional lives. The relationship between artist and agent should be one of employment: the artist employs both the agent and the manager, not the other way round. The artist finds work and pays the agent commission to handle the negotiations and paperwork. The agent may well find work for the artist and may even earn a slightly higher commission for this work, but the hungry artist cannot afford to wait for this to happen.

The true route to success in the voice-over world is to apply directly to the source of work, thereby cutting out all middlemen. The best sources of work to apply to are the ones that pay the most. Why chase a £9 radio commercial when you can go for a £5,125 TV commercial? The effort required is exactly the same in both cases. You make a tape, you make a phone call, you write a letter sending the tape, you do an audition, and . . . you get rejected. Well, maybe not rejected, but certainly not chosen. There is a popular rule of thumb in voice-over circles which says that you have to go through this process at least 20 times before getting a job. The competition for the £9 jobs is no less fierce than the competition for the better paid ones. If you are going to get one job in 20 it makes sense to try for the ones that pay the most!

As you will see in chapter 9, advertising agencies are always eager to find new voices. Yet voice agents are keen to protect the livelihoods of their existing clients and their initial reaction to a non-famous newcomer will be to get them off the phone as quickly as possible. Standard rejections are:

- our books are closed for six months
- we've just had our new CD done so we can't take anyone else on
- we've already got someone who sounds just like you
- we don't take on beginners
- we only handle famous voices.

The last point is a new one and may well be the way voice agencies work in the 21st century. They will be applying the same principle as you should be: if you only get one job in 20, make sure it earns good money. Famous people command higher fees, and 15 per cent commission on higher fees is better than 15 per cent of an unknown's fee. In the very near future voice agencies may well decide not to represent the unknowns.

2

Voices

It is important to know who, in voice terms, you are. Potential employers will be more interested in your 'natural' voice than your impressive range of accents and regional dialects. If you listen to commercials and commentaries you will realise that they fall into a few main categories.

COMMERCIALS

The Hard Sell
Fast talking, hard hitting, usually selling furniture or carpets and nearly always with a 'buy before the end of the month' special offer.

The Soft Sell
The seductive voice purring sexily about fragrances, chocolates, and all things put in or on the body.

The 'Real' Person
The 'real' person sells hair care products, pet foods, financial services, insurance, and female 'unmentionables'.

The Character
The wacky, larger-than-life sort of person you would cross the street to avoid. Sells soft drinks, domestic cleaning products (especially for toilets and carpets), and children's toys and games.

The Announcer
The announcer only ever speaks in the third person and tells us what a fine job a company is doing. Used by large corporations and utility companies providing gas, water, and electricity. The announcer always tries to sound 'official'. Government departments use announcers!

The Spokesperson
Used on behalf of a company and usually locked into the first person plural: we do this, we do that, etc. Home improvement companies selling windows, doors, floors and heating employ spokespersons.

The Gossip
The gossip is usually downmarket and is overheard talking to her friend about the product in question. She is a well-known actress pretending to be a real person. Because she is talking to her friend and not us she is able to say things which we might not otherwise believe. She is stating her opinions, not facts.

COMMENTARIES

Commentaries are the scripts which accompany films, documentaries and audio programmes dealing with history, wildlife, politics, travel, medicine, teaching, finance, and so on. The list is endless.

Financial
Voices for financial subjects fall into two main types. If the film is a company report to shareholders or potential investors, the voice is expected to be very confident with a touch of arrogance. 'We *are* the best' as opposed to 'We are the *best*'. If the film is selling a financial product such as a pension scheme, insurance policy or investment opportunity, a very soothing, reassuring voice is called for.

Investigative
Consumer affairs programmes dealing with matters of public concern like to use a voice with an edge of sarcasm. One effective BBC technique is to give the script to two voices:

Voice 1 We said ...
Voice 2 Is it normal for the wheels to fall off your buses?
Voice 1 And they said ...
Voice 2 Well, we wouldn't say it was normal exactly ...
Voice 1 So we said ...
Voice 2 But you're not surprised that a wheel came off?
Voice 1 And they put the phone down and wouldn't talk to us!

This works very well because the actors are able to inflect the words in a way that tells us whether or not we are dealing with dishonest people, without actually saying anything actionable in a court of law.

Wildlife

The wildlife voice has to fool the listener or viewer into thinking that the script was recorded at the same time as the film was being shot. The effect is easily achieved: talk in a tone of voice that would not frighten the animals away if you really were that close to them – quietly, close to the mic, and very soothing.

Teaching

This voice has to be very calm and reassuring. It must make everything it says sound so simple that you could not possibly get it wrong. However, if you do get it wrong we will just go over it again as many times as you wish. We have infinite patience. We never get cross.

Medical

People usually only access medical information when they, or someone close to them, has something to be concerned about. Patients do not like their doctors to be too young. They like them educated, well modulated, approachable, with plenty of time to talk things through. Medical matters are best dealt with by mature voices.

Technical

When explaining something technical the voice has to 'see' everything it is talking about. This work is best suited to voices with highly developed visualisation skills and good body language.

Travel

The traveller must be adept at pronouncing words and place names in foreign languages. The voice must also be enthusiastic and sound as if it has a sense of humour – necessary when things go wrong. And they always do!

Sport

Sportspeople tend to be a little nasal, and comfortable with convoluted sentences and strange imagery – 'sick as a parrot' being a fine example. It is necessary to be able to change from calmness to absolute hysteria in a matter of seconds.

The Arts

The voices of the arts have polarised into the effete and the professional working class. Some very successful arts voices are so stylised as to be completely unbelievable and unrealistic. However, somebody somewhere believes in them because they crop up all over the place, most noticeably in the world of the theatre-based (but not necessarily theatrical) arts. The professional working class voice seems most at home when commenting on the more avant garde visual arts.

The quickest way to find employment as a voice-over is to present yourself as belonging to one of these cliché groups. The question is – which one?

LOOKING AT SCRIPTS

It is very important to start listening to and recording all sorts of voices. It is equally necessary to transcribe scripts and make notes about the style of delivery. Listen for inflections, pauses and emphases and find a way of marking them in your transcription. The convention is an arrow pointing upwards at 45 degrees for upward inflections, and one pointing downwards at 45 degrees for downward inflections. A vertical line indicates a pause and underlining a word indicates a slight emphasis.

Transcribe scripts of all lengths and styles – from lightweight commercials to political commentaries; from both television and radio. It is important to time commercials. Airtime is sold by the second – usually 10-, 20-, 30-, or 40-second slots, and the timings have to be absolutely accurate. During commercial breaks on radio and television, different areas of the country often have different commercials. These 'splits' are computer controlled and the various regions are reunited after a precisely measured interval. In fact, all commercials run half a second under their agreed time. This creates a slightly smoother transition between consecutive ads. Precise timing is an essential skill in voice-overs. A 30-second script has to be delivered in 29.5 seconds – no more, no less. If you finish two seconds before the end, the client will think he is paying for wasted airtime, or, even worse, that he could have got six more words into the script!

As well as listening to broadcast voice-overs it is very important to listen to yourself. To do this you will need to record your own voice. The minimum equipment necessary to do this is a domestic cassette recorder, a decent but not expensive microphone, and a set of enclosed headphones. The headphones need to cover the ears so that they exclude outside sounds; the 'Walkman' type of headphones are not really suitable but will do if that is all you have. Everything should be available in second-hand shops for about £50 ($80), but many homes will already have a recording tape deck and headphones so all that will be needed is a mic. These can be bought at a reasonable price from specialist electrical stores.

It is also possible to make recordings with a PC – there is a recording programme within Microsoft Windows. The PC can be turned into a very sophisticated recording studio, allowing the mixing and editing of voice, music and effects. The weak link is the mic – it is not possible to plug a high quality mic directly into a computer without using a professional phantom power supply and a pre-amp. A small mixing desk from an electronics shop would provide both of these for about £100 ($160). It is not necessary to have an amp or speakers for either the computer or the tape deck as everything can be listened to through the headphones. The same equipment can be used to record material from the radio or television by putting the mic near the loud speakers.

Most domestic cassette decks feed the signal being recorded to the headphones, so wearing the headphones while speaking into the mic will go some way towards simulating the feel of working in a voice studio. If there is a volume control, set the headphones to be quite loud – so that all you can hear through them is the voice being picked up by the microphone.

Record the scripts that you have transcribed and compare your recordings with the originals. Voice-over is about listening, and the first and most important person to listen to is yourself. You should begin to get some idea of where your voice fits in. Are you hard sell or soft sell, wildlife or sport? It is very important that you decide how to present yourself to prospective employers. Their initial criteria are 'Do we like the voice and how would we categorise it?' If you can make it easy for them to know where to put you – quite literally, where to put your tape on the shelf – you stand a better chance of finding employment. If your particular place on the shelf contains five other similar voices, they might consider it a waste of time and space to house your tape in addition to the others. This is not a rejection – it simply means that, at the moment, they do not need what you have to offer; they've got plenty of it already.

One of the purposes of the recording, listening, and comparing exercise is to discover as soon as possible exactly what your strengths are. Having discovered them, you then have to refine and exploit them.

When listening to your recordings, one of the things you are almost certain to notice is all the noises that accompany your speech. You will hear extraneous domestic sounds in the background – traffic, radio, TV, other people, children, etc. – and you will probably become aware of the sound and pattern of your own breathing. How and when to breathe are important decisions which have to be taken for every script. In almost every case they are different. When you start out you will probably sound as if you are running a race and taking many shallow breaths. This is called panic breathing. You take a small breath at every possible occasion and then suddenly you say 'I'm running out of breath' and exhale a lungful of air. If you are out of breath, why are you exhaling?

Taking a lot of shallow breaths actually overinflates the lungs until they can take no more and you exhale noisily. Panic breathing is a natural reaction in stressful situations. The voice-over artist has to learn to overcome this reaction. The best and most natural breathers are babies. If you want to know how to breathe correctly, look at a baby. They breathe deeply and slowly and appear to inflate the stomach. This is called diaphragmatic breathing. They are not inflating the stomach, however; what you can see is the movement of the diaphragm which causes air to be drawn in to the bottom of the lungs. Men spend a lot of time 'holding themselves in' in order not to look overweight. Diaphragmatic breathing can make them look as if they have an expanding waistline – so they don't do it! Instead, most men adopt the army stance of head up, chest out, stomach in, standing stiffly to attention. This is completely wrong for voice-overs. An excellent place to learn, in fact relearn, diaphragmatic breathing is in yoga classes.

Before starting a script, stand still and take two or three deep breaths, distending the stomach and keeping the shoulders down. Hold one of these breaths for two seconds and then start one of your chosen scripts. Many people start a script immediately after a huge snatched in-breath. This sounds terrible and communicates a sense of panic to the listener. Some radio journalists prefix each recording by counting '5, 4, 3, 2, 1' and taking a snatched panic breath. This does not work either. The engineer will be grateful for two seconds of silence before you start. Snatched panic breaths have to be edited off the start of recordings and sometimes this can be quite hard to do. Very often the panic in-breath is joined to the first word of the script and it is not possible to separate the two and end up with a natural-sounding result. This is particularly noticeable on news programmes on smaller radio stations where a report has been very clumsily edited – if you hear a rapid sucking sound at the beginning or end of a piece it is probably a panic breath that has not been properly removed.

Some people make noises other than breathing, when they speak. A dry mouth causes clicking sounds rather like those made by a noisy eater. Keeping the mouth moist by sipping water will help stop this. Sticky lips can make noises and these can be cured by the regular application of lip salve or Vaseline. These noises are more noticeable on recordings made when speaking quietly, close to the mic. If there is no cure and they cannot be edited out, the only solution is to disguise them by playing the sound of a mountain stream underneath the voice. It is surprising how many 'sexy-voiced' commercials contain the sound of running water!

When listening to your recorded voice you may become aware of idiosyncrasies that you have not noticed before. These can restrict your chances of employment. Stuttering is the one most likely to preclude you from a career in voice-overs. However, some people who stutter do not do so when speaking in an assumed voice. If your natural speech includes a stutter it might be worth creating an alter ego in voice and name who does not stutter. A lazy 'r' which comes out as a 'w' can restrict you to comedy parts. These conditions might be helped by courses of lessons with specialist voice teachers.

Asthmatics are also unlikely to be employed for straight voice-overs. The microphone will pick up wheezing sounds very clearly. It is very hard to predict when a wheezing attack will occur; a trip to the studio in cold, frosty air can trigger one, as can a particularly strong perfume or aftershave. On the other hand, wheeziness might be capitalised on by specialising in the voices of rheumy old men or women.

The voice-over artist has to keep the face, tongue and mouth in peak condition. The best way to do this is to use them by reading aloud as often as possible. A musician knows that the only way to master a difficult piece of music is to play it out loud. Similarly, the only way to practise a voice-over script is to read it out loud. Muttering things under your breath may help the eye–brain co-ordination but it does nothing for the muscles that actually do the work. Complicated words and sequences of words have to be lodged in the muscle memory as well as the brain. The biggest single mistake made by voice-over artists is not practising out loud in the studio. Some see it as demeaning to admit that they need to practise something, and so they go on making the same mistakes to the exasperation of all concerned. If your client sees you trying the script out loud and running over difficult sections they will be impressed by your professionalism. Sitting in the corner reading the paper impresses no-one! One very good exercise for both beginners and seasoned pros is to read (out loud) with the teeth clenched together.

As well as being exercised, the voice needs to be taken care of. Smoking, either active or passive, is bad for the voice. This is a controversial subject amongst voice artists. Most studios and associated areas in the voice world are strictly non-smoking, however, deep, husky-voiced voice-overs of both sexes often say that smoking helped create their unique sound, and so they are not prepared to risk destroying their livelihood by stopping. The irony is that continuing to smoke will certainly render them unemployable (or dead) before long.

Diet can also affect the voice. Dairy products cause the body to create mucus which lurks in the chest and nasal passages. Mucus can make a voice sound very nasal and blocked. It can be cleared by blowing the nose, sniffing or spitting, but it has a habit of returning in mid-sentence and completely changing the resonance of the voice. It is most noticeable on the 'n' sounds as it turns them into 'd' sounds. Tea, coffee and other drinks containing caffeine can have a similar effect. The answer is to avoid them for 24 hours before a recording session. If you become a busy professional you may well have to avoid them completely. Many voice-over artists arrive at a session with their own herbal tea bags and accept only a cup of hot water when drinks are offered. As well as creating mucus, caffeinated drinks increase the heart rate and induce a state of anxiety which is not desirable when recording. Alternative therapists say that drinking pineapple juice can have a very beneficial effect on the voice.

The voice is created within the body and so it follows that the body is the only thing which can modify or change the voice. Control of the relationship between body and voice is one of the most important and difficult skills to be mastered by anyone wishing to do this work. The ultimate technical aim of all voice artists must be to have complete control over the voice and for it to perform any pitch shift or inflection asked of it. This sounds as if it should happen naturally, but my experience is that even those fairly busy in the voice world have a surprising lack of control.

When confronted with a script and a microphone most people resort to using downward inflections on key words and at the end of sentences. They do not do this in normal speech. In everyday conversation the downward inflection is a sign that the speaker has finished and it is the turn of the other person to say something. It may also signify disapproval or depression. None of these things have a place in commercials and are not often heard in well-performed commentaries and voice-overs.

The listener has to be seduced into listening, engaged by what he or she is hearing, and manipulated into continuing to listen until such time as the voice-over signals that it is time to stop. To achieve this the voice artist constructs an architecture of pitches and inflections which carry the listener along on a magic carpet of words, bringing them gently back to earth at the end of the message.

The secret of achieving this control lies in the use of the body. When we listen to a good voice-over what we are actually listening to is good audible body language. Recent research has shown that voice and gesture are controlled by exactly the same part of the brain. The human body is said to have a potential of 700,000 different gestures; get the gesture right and the voice will follow – without having to think about it. It will sound natural rather than contrived.

13

The most common male stance in front of the microphone is with the hands in the pockets. When challenged about this the hands will be taken out of the pockets and clasped in front of the genitals. If this is challenged they will be clasped behind the back over the bottom. After this they will be crossed over the chest. In body language terms these are all defensive positions. Women go through a similar pattern of behaviour (although if they do not have pockets the first stage is omitted). The speaker displaying this body language is 'hiding' and is in no mood to communicate. They are, for some reason, embarrassed. What is needed is a firm, rooted stance in front of the microphone, the hands poised for action, ready to point out the things to be talked about – be they concrete or abstract.

If you have any lingering doubt or scepticism about the importance of body language to voice-overs, please consider this: the loudest thing on tape is a smile!

3

Voice Meets Script

Voice-overs are not normally improvised; they follow a script. One of the most effective commercial scripts ever written is: *Tomorrow morning – all brand new cars half price!* The message is so simple and so electrifying that anybody with an intelligible voice could be booked to read it. No special inflections or pitch patterns are needed and sound effects or music are completely unnecessary. This, however, is an exceptional situation. Advertising scripts usually offer products or services which are not immediately desirable. In order to deliver their message they have to engage the attention of the listener and then keep it.

Sex appears to be of interest to most people so starting a commercial with the question: *Did you get it last night?* might be considered to be an attention grabber provided that the delivery is husky, close to the microphone, and laden with innuendo. The voice artist walking into a studio and being handed a piece of paper with: *Did you get it last night?* written on it needs to know a little background information before saying anything. It is vitally important to know the who, how, what, when, where and why of a script.

WHO AM I?

Famous people are booked to be themselves. Everybody else needs to know who they are to be – announcer, salesman, seducer, motorist, cook, husband, teenager, housewife, gossip, advisor, character, spokesman or tagman.

WHO AM I TALKING TO?

A very important question, but one which is not asked often enough. A woman asking the question: *Did you get it last night?* uses a different inflection depending on who she is talking to. If it is directed at another woman there is an element of sisterly confidentiality. If it is directed at a man it will be teasingly seductive.

HOW FAST AM I SAYING IT?

Time is of the essence in commercials. It is important to establish the time available for the delivery of a script. The length of a commercial is usually written at the top of the page, but this may not be the length of the script. A 30-second commercial might be 25 seconds of script and 5 seconds of jingle. It is important to ensure that the script fills the time available without sounding rushed. It may be far too wordy – clients always want to convey as much information as possible for their money. The very best commercials have only a few well-chosen words delivered in a memorable style.

When a beginner tries to fit a script into a pre-determined time there are two approaches: start as fast as possible and slow down, or start slowly and gradually speed up. Starting too fast removes the psychological barrier of wondering if you can fit it into the time available, but it can be difficult to slow down; starting slow and speeding up can sound 'panicked', with a tendency to rush in order to finish on time. My experience, as a director, is that the best method is to start slowly without reference to the clock and get the voice artist to speed up by giving them a reason to do so other than time. So I might suggest that a script is delivered more 'urgently' rather than just faster. 'Urgent' is a better motivation than 'fast'.

HOW AM I SAYING IT?

Seductively in this case. But it could be angrily: *You've forgotten to get it for the past three days and you promised you'd get it on the way home and I'm fed up, so did you get it last night?* You could equally be inquisitive, bored, excited, pleased, miserable or suspicious. Try saying the phrase and shifting the emphasis on to each word in turn.

> <u>Did</u> you get it last night?
> Did <u>you</u> get it last night?
> Did you <u>get</u> it last night?
> Did you get <u>it</u> last night?
> Did you get it <u>last</u> night?
> Did you get it last <u>night</u>?

Each one of these phrases has an entirely different meaning. If you then repeat the exercise choosing various people from the 'Who am I?' category you can see that the possible permutations of character and meaning are endless.

WHAT AM I SAYING?

Commercials are very carefully designed to avoid saying something they don't mean. On the other hand, many advertisers are only too keen to mean something that they don't say. They may not be able to say what they would like to for legal reasons or for fear of offending public morals or taste. Commercial scripts are submitted for legal approval in writing, and there are many scripts which have appeared perfectly acceptable on the printed page but which have taken on entirely new meanings when recorded by a skilled voice artist. As we saw at the beginning of the book: *Chocolates! It shows how much you care* can have two entirely different meanings. In the world of advertising, coffee seems to be associated with sexual liaisons – promised or failed. The popular end-of-date question 'Are you coming in for a coffee?' has very little to do with the slaking of thirst. Advertisers have realised this and mini-soap operas have been created around coffee commercials. If we now prefix our phrase with 'coffee' we get: *Coffee? Did you get it last night?* This expands the range of possible meanings enormously.

It is important to be very clear exactly what it is you are 'saying' before launching yourself on such a seemingly innocuous phrase.

WHAT AM I FEELING?

This is very important for 'real person' spots. Are you happy, sad, reflective, excited, tired or apprehensive?

WHAT AM I DOING?

Particularly important for 'real person' spots on radio. Are you riding, driving, walking, drinking, socialising, dreaming, boasting, seducing, eating or window shopping?

WHEN AM I SAYING IT?

The position of a line within a commercial script will affect its delivery. The opening line is designed to arouse the interest of the listener. Many of them are questions, such as: *Ladies, is there a bonking under your bonnet?* or *Do you know the secret of the Black Magic box?* These are very cleverly worded questions designed to make people listen to whatever comes next. They usually have a pay-off or resolution right at the end of the commercial which is designed to stick in the memory. It may be catchy because of the way it is delivered or it may be another clever use of words.

Here are the last lines of the two opening questions above:

Ladies, is there a bonking under your bonnet? ends with a rather jaunty *MAK Car Care Centres – we'll sort you out. No problem!*

and:

Do you know the secret of the Black Magic box? finishes very ambiguously with: *Black Magic, your secret's safe with us!*

So *Did you get it last night* at the beginning of a script could be a straight question, seductive, caring, laden with comic innuendo, or cheeky. At the end of the script it could still be all of those things but must now be memorable, designed to stick in the memory like a catchphrase. Ideally, 'Did you get it last night?' should pass into everyday language, thus keeping the product in the public consciousness.

The closing phrase of a commercial is known as the tag. If the opening and the closing are performed by one voice and the middle by a second voice, the middle section is known as a doughnut (or in the USA as a donut).

WHEN WILL IT BE BROADCAST?

Most national commercials are booked to be broadcast at very specific times. A script to be broadcast at breakfast time should sound different from a late night script. Regional television and radio commercials are usually booked on a blanket basis, where the station guarantees to broadcast it an agreed number of times per day with a couple of spots at peak time so the voice has to be suitable for all hours of the day or night.

WHERE AM I SAYING IT?

It is important to know where the commercial is set, particularly for radio commercials. Television voice-overs tend to be just that – a voice over the action. Radio voices can be 'set' anywhere – in a pub, factory, staff room, kitchen, bed, swimming pool or garden. Knowing where you are changes the energy of the delivery.

WHY AM I SAYING IT?

Is the script a public health warning, sale announcement, trailer, promo, special offer, charity appeal, last-minute reminder or investment opportunity? They should all sound different.

Obviously an experienced voice-over does not arrive at a studio with a list of prepared questions, all of which have to have satisfactory answers before they will open their mouth. The process

18

becomes instinctive. You learn to look at a script and know which are the relevant questions to ask. Asking questions endears you to the client and the creative team. The worst thing you can do is take a script and perform it without asking for guidance. You need to know how they imagine it being read. The client (who likes to be involved) and the creative team often see the voice-over as the icing on the cake of a commercial. It is the part of a commercial that has the greatest impact. People who read the paper or get a drink during commercial breaks on television can still be reached by the voice-over. It can still get the message across and, best of all, it might entice the errant viewer back to watch the commercial.

The script is precious; it is a baby conceived by a creative individual and brought into the world by a committee. The final version of a script is not usually entrusted to one person. It is arrived at after a seemingly endless series of meetings, consultations and approvals. Advertising agencies always date each version of a script and, to avoid misunderstandings and mistakes, give it a 'version' or 'revision' number. This information usually appears at the top of the page of a script. Version or revision numbers in double figures indicate a particularly difficult birthing process. A wise voice-over artist never comments on the quality of a script. Remarks such as 'Who wrote this rubbish' are best left unsaid.

Instead of being improved, scripts sometimes get worse as they progress through different versions. One person's inspirational concept is butchered beyond recognition by the creative committee. The client wants as much information as possible while the creative director favours an arty, minimalist approach. The result, an inevitable compromise, satisfies neither party and the voice artist has to pick up the pieces and turn a sow's ear into a silk purse!

When we go to the theatre or cinema, or watch television, we subscribe to a 'willing suspension of disbelief'. We say to ourselves, 'I am going to watch actors performing a story. I will see illusion presented as reality and the reality of my surroundings will be replaced by the illusion of the story. For the duration of the performance I will believe in the reality of the illusion.'

The willing suspension of disbelief does not extend to commercials. If acting is about 'truth' then commercials are about 'lying'. All broadcast scripts have to be legally approved by the regulatory authorities and all claims, comparisons, statistics and examples have to be proved to be accurate. However, contrary to the subtle suggestions of most commercials, the average person knows that he or she does not need a new perfume, deodorant, floor cleaner, insurance policy or cat food. Advertising has been defined as 'taking away people's sense of security and self-respect and selling it back to them at a price'. The most important quality for a commercial voice-over is to be believable, however it is not the message that has to be believed but the voice saying it. It isn't *what* you say that counts, it's *how* you say it! Of course this is a terrible generalisation but it's no good saying, 'This is the best floor cleaner money can buy' if you don't sound as if you believe it yourself.

COMMERCIAL SCRIPTS

The secret of good commercial delivery lies in the three Ps – pitch, pace and pauses.

Pitch

There should be a very definite architecture of pitches within every commercial – not just a steady monotone or random rising and falling of the voice. The worst and least effective delivery is one which follows a descending pitch pattern. If you read: *This is the best floor cleaner money can buy* with every word being at a slightly lower pitch than the one before it, you end up with a very negative statement which is definitely not going to sell floor cleaner! The words at the beginning of a script need to engage the listener and encourage them to keep listening. The best way to do this is to use an absolutely startling statement, such as: *Tomorrow morning all brand new cars half price!* Less effective scripts need subtle pitch changes to make them interesting. The most effective delivery of an otherwise dull script is achieved by starting with an ascending pitch pattern. Raising the pitch of each successive word can sound false at the beginning of a commercial but surprisingly memorable at the end.

At the beginning of a script it is often better to raise the pitch of successive groups of words. It is essential to identify the most important word or words in the statement. Taken as a statement in isolation and without reference to pictures or images which may accompany it (or to anything which may come before or after), the most important words are *floor cleaner*. They are the subject of the statement and the listener needs to know what you are talking about. On stage or in normal speech we might use volume to create this emphasis. This is not possible in voice-overs as the master recording is electronically compressed to iron out any highs or lows in volume. For a commercial to be effective in a noisy car driving at high speed on a busy motorway all the words need to be as loud as possible. Thus the best way to create emphasis is to raise the pitch of the important words.

This is the best is on one pitch; *floor cleaner* is slightly higher; *money* drops back to the original pitch; *can* is higher; and *buy* is higher still. This creates a plausible delivery with the voice sounding committed to the message.

Many people find this precise pitching of words extremely difficult. In normal speech they would do it without thinking but the presence of a microphone seems to have a magical effect on pitch patterns – they all spiral downwards. Directing people to raise the pitch of a particular word – insisting that they do so – can cause great frustration, anger and upset. Even the most experienced voice artist gets into the habit of using descending pitches and they often need to hear their recordings before accepting that they are doing it. The anger and frustration come from the realisation that they do not have as much control over their voice as they would like. The first thing in life that babies do is to breath in, and the second is (usually) to use their voice to cry or make a noise. From that moment on the voice 'works'. It does not need language because the simple use of sound gets the baby fed, changed, played with, put to sleep and cuddled. Suddenly, to discover in later life that you have very little control over the use of precise variations in pitch can be a very unsettling experience. It is not an easy skill to master. Musicians are particularly good at it, however, as their early training in which they are taught to 'hear' or sing a note before playing it, gives them a good understanding of the subtleties of pitch. Many successful voice-over artists come from a musical rather than an acting background.

Using an upward inflection is a psychologically exposed action and some part of the brain appears to block it. Some people find it almost impossible to say, for example, *Bombay Sapphire*, with the second word at a slightly higher pitch than the first. Others can do it but sound like a computer speech generator. There are two ways to overcome this block – word substitution and gesture.

Word Substitution

We employ the most delicate and subtle pitch shifts and pauses when embarking on matters carnal. The negotiation of the start of a sexual relationship is like a very delicate and precise dance. Ordinary words like 'coffee' become laden with innuendo. Innocent phrases such as 'I suppose I'd better be going home now' beg for the 'Well, you don't have to' response. Direct eye contact is avoided and both parties stare moodily at the same object while one of them runs their finger up and down it in a subconsciously erotic gesture.

Harnessing this subtlety can open the doors to skilful control of the voice. When directing someone who is having problems achieving a subtly rising inflection, I encourage them to use substitutions. I ask people to think of the words they might use to describe someone they consider to be sexually attractive. These may be kept as secret and unspoken words or they may be said aloud, but they will inevitably contain a rising inflection. The rising inflections used in the context of sexual attraction are much more subtle than those used in questions – this is how we recognise them as being part of the coded language more commonly described as innuendo. Once the special words have been decided upon it is necessary to transfer their inflection to the relevant words in the script – in this case *Bombay Sapphire*. This is best done by repeating the 'sexy words' followed by *Bombay Sapphire* until the inflexion has moved across.

Obviously the actual words used for substitution vary from person to person, and it is worth finding out in advance what it is that will create the desired effect for you. Some of the more long-serving members of the voice-over community use the phrase 'nice car' to get themselves in the mood for the hard sell slots. They repeat it five or six times with increasing aggression before launching themselves into the script.

Gesture

Gesture and voice pitch are very closely linked. They are both controlled by the same part of the brain. If, during normal speech, we point upwards, the voice pitch rises; if we point downwards it falls. For a voice-over to be believable it cannot simply be read aloud – there must be a large physical involvement with what the script is saying. When saying *Bombay* point to the bottle, then point to something a little higher when saying *Sapphire*. This should produce the required upward change in pitch. At first this process produces large jumps in pitch, but, with practice, the brain learns to make very small but very effective pitch changes. With any luck it will become less shy and stop blocking the rising inflection.

In a commercial, the pitches should flow gracefully so that the listener is not aware of what is going on. The voice should be like a magic carpet, transporting the listener from one end of the script to the other, giving them something to think about on the way and something to remember when it has brought them safely back to earth again. One way of achieving a smooth flow is to perform graceful and flowing movements with the hands when delivering the script – rather like pretend T'ai Chi. Fast-moving and punchy commercials like those selling furniture or announcing amazing warehouse sales require a very different physical approach, however. Short, sharp jabbing and pointing movements give a script energy and hammer home important points. These scripts use very jerky pitch changes – there is nothing graceful about them.

Pace

Pace is the speed, or the perceived speed, of the delivery. All that rushes is not fast! Pace is not the time taken for a script or part of a script. By giving individual words a lot of energy and by making sure that every one is isolated from the next it is possible to record a script which feels as if it is fast and energetic but which proceeds at exactly the speed necessary for the assimilation of the information being given.

Today's the day that Dreams and Desires open their latest designer outlet at Warehouse West.

This opening line of 15 words occupies exactly four seconds. For it to be understandable, energetic and interesting it has to be given a very staccato delivery with an infinitely small silence between each word.

Have you noticed unwanted lines and wrinkles around your eyes and mouth?

This also lasts for four seconds and, at 12 words, is nearly as long as the previous example. It should have an air of discretion and confidentiality and a very relaxed feeling – we are mentioning delicate and potentially embarrassing matters. If it is spoken with gaps between the words it will sound very stilted and awkward; the delivery has to be smooth with the words very slightly running into each other. Technically this is known as eliding the words, which is the equivalent of legato in music. By eliminating the gaps and therefore being able to lengthen the words very slightly, a much more relaxed feeling is created.

Pause

Pauses frighten inexperienced voice-over artists as, like upward inflections, they are very exposed. However, pauses make people listen. A good school teacher is able to regain the interest of the daydreamer by pausing. In the classroom the most reassuring sound is the steady drone of a boring teacher – they are in their little world, as are most of the class. They do not intrude on each other. However, if the teacher pauses in mid-sentence, especially in an unexpected place, the daydreamers are jolted into panicked attention. The teacher might be looking at them or, even worse, might have just asked them a question! So they sit up and take notice.

Do you know the secret of the Black Magic Box?
No!
Then I'll tell you.

These, the first three lines of a very famous commercial, rely on pauses to increase their effectiveness and make them even more tantalising. The first line is a question asked with seductive intent. It is followed by a pause. The *No* tells us that the answer was in the negative and that the questioner was both surprised and excited by it, so there is an erotic pause after it. *Then I'll tell you* expresses the thinly disguised excitement at having at last found a Black Magic virgin on which to practise his or her wicked desires. The whole Black Magic script is dealt with in greater detail in chapter 4.

Once the three Ps have been sorted out there are many other equally important things to look out for in a commercial script:

Added value words

'Added value' words are an important part of commercial script writing and must therefore be an important feature in the delivery of the script. They too are emphasised by isolating them with pauses. Common added value words include: *and, plus, more, free, new, real, next, improved.*

> With <u>free</u> next day deliveries for any order over £30 Viking Direct offers superb value.

> Buy before the end of the month <u>and</u> we'll give you free delivery <u>plus</u> 2 years extended warranty.

As well as putting a small pause either side of these words, their pitch should be very slightly raised for added emphasis.

Questions Posed

Make sure they really do sound like questions, with a rise in pitch at the end of the sentence: *Are you paying too much for your car insurance?*

Questions such as this at the start of a commercial really grab the listener's attention – everybody thinks they are paying too much for their car insurance. But, for it to work, the question really hasto sound like a question and not like a statement. Many commercials do start with questions rather than statements because they exploit the listener's doubts and insecurities.

Solutions Offered

Any commercial posing a question must also offer a solution. The solution invariably comes at the end of the commercial and follows a repetition of the question: *So, if you are paying too much for your car insurance, call Infinity Brokers on 08000 735 537.*

If the question poses a problem or raises a doubt, the solution offered must have the feel of the US Cavalry galloping over the horizon.

Memorable Hooks

These can be either catchphrases which stick in the memory or a quirky way of pronouncing the product name.

When it comes to boats – we don't mess about! is used by one company offering boating holidays and is, of course, reminiscent of the song 'Messing About On The River'. This has to be delivered with a conspiratorial wink, which lets the listener know that it is a deliberately silly catchphrase. Winking after *boats* and smiling through *we don't mess about* will produce the desired effect.

N N N Nutalls! is the quirky way one toffee manufacturer likes to advertise its name. This benefits from the employment of a cartoon-like voice.

Statutory Words

These are words which have to be included in a commercial for legal reasons. During television commercials they appear in vision, usually superimposed over the last shot. In radio commercials this is not possible and so they have to be spoken. The number of statutory words that used to have to be included in commercials for financial services in the UK grew so large that on many occasions they occupied more time than the selling. However, much to everyone's relief, the regulations in the UK were relaxed in the summer of 2000. Here are some of the ones you are still likely to come across.

For medicines: *Always read the label* and *If symptoms persist consult a qualified medical practitioner.*

For financial services: *The value of your investments can go down as well as up.*

For mortgages: *Your home is at risk if you do not keep up payments on loans secured on it.*

For ads offering credit: *Written credit details on request.*

For special offers: *Terms and conditions apply – see pack for details.*

Advertisers do not like having to include statutory words in commercials because they break the flow or ruin an illusion. They also take up valuable airtime which has to be paid for. The only way of dealing with them is to say them as quickly as possible, consistent with maintaining clarity. They should have a throwaway feel to them. It is worth practising these at speed so that they can be easily dealt with when they occur.

Paravocal Communication

These are the sounds that we make and use but which are not words even though they do convey meaning. Here are some examples:

- smacking the lips when you see something appetising
- the 'tsk, tsk' of disapproval
- clearing the throat to signal the telling of an untruth
- the sharp intake of breath that denotes shock or surprise
- the exhaled blow of exasperation.

All these sounds are used in commercials and can be very powerful methods of communicating things that would not be allowed to be said in words.

The Positive Negative

Many commercials make negative statements, but as advertising is the land of the relentlessly positive they too have to become positives.

I don't want to worry about how my hair looks appears to be a negative statement but it has to sound positive. The way to achieve this is to deliver it with a broad smile and raised eyebrows. This is very positive body language and has a powerful effect on the spoken word. It makes it almost impossible to do a downward inflection. Body language is clearly audible even though the listener may not be aware of it. We have spent so much time talking on the telephone that, unknowingly, we have learned to identify the 'sound' of body language. We can tell if someone is lying down, impatient, ill, unhappy, and very often we can tell if they are lying. In voice-overs it is really important to achieve the appropriate body language.

This is a commercial for a product we really don't want you to buy!

Who makes a commercial for any other reason than to get a positive response? In this case they do want you to buy the product but, as they are advertising a medication, they are expressing sympathy that your condition is such that you need to buy it! So this statement has to be very positive.

Telephone Numbers

The telephone number is one of the most important elements in many commercials. It is the means by which the listener can contact the company in order to buy the goods or services on offer. It has to be delivered in a way that not only makes it memorable but persuades the listener that even they can remember it.

In the UK the word 'zero' is not used in telephone numbers. The number 0 is pronounced as 'oh'. The number 88 can be spoken as 'eighty eight' or 'double eight'; 88 44 88 is better as 'double eight double four double eight' than 'eighty eight forty four eighty eight'. The use of 'double' is mostly confined to the UK as people from other English-speaking countries find it confusing. Referring to a number which is repeated three times, such as 888, as 'treble eight' is now very rare.

Dialling codes such as 0800 and 05000 are delivered as 'oh eight hundred' and 'oh five thousand' in the UK, and 'zero eight hundred' and 'zero five thousand' in other countries. In the USA, 212 is 'two one two' and not 'two hundred and twelve' or 'two twelve'. There are also numbers which start with a numeric area code and finish with a word which can be picked out from the telephone keypad. A good example in the UK is 07000 1 VOICE.

Some companies find an idiosyncratic and memorable way to phrase their number. The insurance company with the number 555555 shuns 'double five double five double five' and uses the very clever 'five fifty five, five fifty five'. This works very well for them as their commercials are delivered in a very 'upper crust' English accent.

Freephone 0800 42 44 44 is the phone number of a company called Viking Direct. The whole commercial features in the next chapter.

The prefix 'Freephone' reinforces the fact that the call is free, and should be said with a smile; 0800 is 'oh eight hundred'; the number (said as 'forty two, forty four, forty four') should have a descending pitch (surprisingly) with the last 'four' pitched up to the same pitch as the first 'forty'. This delivery is both memorable and simple.

Companies that advertise on radio and have specially written jingles may find that singing the telephone number proves to be the most effective way of making a number memorable. There is a good example of this in the MAK Car Care Centre commercial which is dealt with in the next chapter and is featured on the CD.

Telephone numbers are a minefield! Companies, creative directors and commercial directors all have their own ideas as to what is memorable. It is safest to ask how the phone number should be given before reading it out loud. If you decide to do it in a way which *you* like but which the client does not accept, it can be very hard to change the delivery. Your version was undoubtedly best (or so you think) and it is sometimes difficult to change to something you do not agree with. If this does happen the answer is to write down the new way of delivering it in words rather than figures.

Punctuation

Punctuation can be a hindrance as it is usually incorrectly used and, if observed, breaks the flow of a good script. Capital letters are useful for the voice-over artist as they alert you to proper nouns and new thoughts. Dashes are useful because they signify a pause – but not a break in the thought process. If in doubt it is best to concentrate on making sense of the script and ignore the punctuation.

Some scripts are written entirely in capital letters which makes them extremely difficult to interpret. The use of all capitals usually means that the client wants a forceful delivery and can only think of this way of expressing the desire. The solution is to smile sweetly and get on with the job. Next time you get a booking from the offender call them in advance and ask for the script to be written in a more conventional manner. Make it sound as if you have an eye condition which makes scripts written in capitals difficult to read; it is not wise to make statements which put your client or employer in the wrong!

Layout of the Script
One very important thing to look for in a script is whether it is for radio or television. It will probably say so at the top of the script, but there is one basic difference between the two: radio scripts consist of a piece of paper with the words on, while television scripts are split into two vertical columns. On the left hand side are the visuals described in words, and on the right hand side the script is split into sections to coincide with the appropriate visuals. This can make them difficult to read.

It may be necessary to work harder on a radio script to make the images a little more 'visual'. Using the appropriate body language is the easiest and quickest way of achieving this. Television scripts tell you exactly what the visuals are so you can be more descriptive and supportive of the image.

Paragraph breaks usually signify new thoughts or new pieces of information so they can be attacked with renewed energy.

NARRATION SCRIPTS

A 'narration' script may be for a wildlife programme, a political documentary or public information film, or a video extolling the virtues of a particular product or company. They are not usually advertising or selling in the same way as commercials but, if they are, they are much more subtle in approach. A film made to persuade people to fit smoke alarms in their homes is selling something. In this case it is selling safety. If the film had been made by a smoke alarm manufacturer, out of the goodness of their hearts, they would be very unlikely to feature a product from a rival manufacturer! They will make sure that their own brand is featured prominently and the camera is almost certain to dwell lovingly on their logo and probably their phone number as well!

BATES DORLAND

RADIO SCRIPT

Client: **SAFEWAY**   Ref.:   **AM/DD**

Product: **DEMOLITION DEALS**   Script Date: **5th October 1999**

Title: **DEMO BALL**   Revision No: _____

Length: **30**   Agency Contact: _____

SFX: Building site. Creaking crane.

MVO: [Yelling above the noise] Look out for this week's demolition deals.

SFX: Demolition ball crashing into concrete.

MVO: McCain oven chips reduced from £1.75 to only 99p.

SFX: Demolition ball crashing into concrete.

MVO: 80 Tetley tea bags reduced from £1.69 to only 59p.

SFX: Demolition ball crashing into concrete.

MVO: You'll find lots more demolition deals throughout the store. Offers end Tuesday 15th.

SFX: Demolition ball crashing into concrete.

Approved by:

Creative Director_____   Planning Director _____

Exec CD _____   Head of Television _____

BAD _____   Client _____ Date _____

A typical Radio script. The sound effects (SFX) are interspersed with the spoken words. MVO refers to a male voice-over. FVO would be female. Notice how much information can be gleaned from the page – title, length, style of delivery, medium (radio or TV), date of writing, and number of revisions to the script. Six different people will have given their approval before the script is broadcast.

B A T E S U K

TELEVISION SCRIPT

Client:	**SAFEWAY**	Ref.:	**AM/DD**
Product:	**PRICE CUT '99**	Date:	**3 JUNE 1999**
Title:	**SCISSORS**	Revision No:	**3**
Length:	**20**	Agency Contact:	

VISION

SOUND

Open at home on our little boy in the hallway. He puts on a baseball cap with the name ADAM on it. Through the door to the kitchen we can see mum with the shopping.

MVO: At Safeway, we're dedicated to permanently cutting the cost of raising a family.

Cut to close up on the boy as he checks himself in the mirror.

BOY: Well, I do have impeccable tastes you know.

Cut to close up on a shopping bag with Price Cut '99 logo.

MVO: So with Price Cut '99 we're cutting our prices on the things your family love.

Cut to the boy holding a pair of kiddies blue scissors in one hand and a packet of macaroni in the other. The packet has a small square cut from it from which the macaroni is pouring out.

BOY: Look, I've been doing some Price Cuts of my own.

Super Safeway logo. Price Cut logo and title Lightening the Load.

MVO: Safeway Price Cut '99. Permanently low prices.

Approved by

Creative Director _____

Exec CD _____

BAD _____

Planning Director _____ H OF TV _____

JW _____ JS _____ GH _____

Client _____ Date _____

A typical TV script in its 3rd revision. It is written for a Male voice-over and a boy. The left hand column details the 'visuals' and the script is in the right hand column. The boy appears in the commercial and the MVO is unseen.

Some films are made for charities as fund-raising ventures. But however worthy the cause, the charity concerned is still trying to sell itself as one to which the viewer might like to contribute money. The only films that are not selling something are probably home movies! Television documentaries can be extremely interesting but, in the final analysis, they are made to attract and retain viewers. The BBC has to justify its licence fee by drawing large audiences, and the commercial companies have to attract equally large audiences in order to generate the advertising income on which they depend for their survival.

Most films requiring narration are not made for broadcasting. They may be company reports to shareholders, product information films for retailers, medical information films, product demonstrations for use in do-it-yourself stores, staff training programmes, company profiles for use in exhibitions; the list is endless.

Given that all narrations are, to some extent, selling something, the techniques and tricks used in the delivery of commercials can be applied to them as well. The three Ps – pitch, pace and pause – continue to be extremely important, but in the land of narration there is a new one to add to the list – place.

Place

It is wrongly assumed that voice-overs must be performed by actors because 'acting' is the magic ingredient that makes them believable and interesting. In my experience, 'acting' is the one thing that does *not* make them either interesting or believable. Acting during a voice-over can sound completely false. The exception is where a script calls for the strong characterisation of, for example, an old crone, an upper class silly-ass, a malicious alien, or a mythical creature or beast. It is necessary to act the character, but if you act the character acting the voice-over script you are in serious trouble!

What does work is *re*acting! The voice artist has to create a virtual world in which the content of the script exists, inhabit that world, and then react to the surroundings in which he finds himself. I said earlier that voice-over is a physical medium. It is also a very visual medium. Irrespective of whether the recording is for audio use or for use with pictures and images, it has to create a picture in the mind of the listener. The job of the voice-over artist performing a narrative script is to create a picture in the mind of the listener and give them the time and space to look at it. The only way this can be achieved is if the voice-over first 'sees' their own picture. This may be the wrong picture and will certainly not be the same one as seen by the listener, but the fact that the picture exists communicates itself to the listener and they start to generate their own.

31

When we do not understand something that is being explained to us we often say, 'I can't see it'. When we do understand we say, 'Yes, I see!' We use the expression 'In my mind's eye' to describe this ability to create visual images for abstracts. Listeners need to see!

If the performer has created a virtual world, he or she can react to it by 'looking' at the different elements of it as they are mentioned in the script. Objects can be pointed to – tall ones will naturally be referred to in a higher pitched voice than low ones. Things on the left will be identified by a slightly different voice quality from those on the right. If, in the script, we go from 'here' to 'there', the speaker's head must move from 'here' to 'there' as they describe what is happening. These movements do not have to be great and it is important that the voice does not sound as if it is going 'off mic'.

When the voice-over artist moves his head to 'look' at things, the distance of the mouth from the microphone changes. This creates a small but subconsciously detectable difference in the sound. The listener hears this changing sound and knows that it is caused by the movement of the speaker's head. This movement reveals that there must be something to look at and therefore the listener 'believes' the speaker and starts to see their own version of the pictures.

Everything referred to is given a 'place'. It may sound complicated and even a little esoteric but it is exactly what we do in everyday speech without thinking about it. An aeroplane flies in the sky so we refer to it in a higher pitched voice than we would a submarine which travels under the ocean. *Look, there's an aeroplane* has a high pitched ending, while *Look, there's a submarine* has a low pitched ending.

The following is an extract from a travelogue:

The Portuguese capital is truly a city of contrasts where you will find a combination of new and old, with fashionable shopping areas, fine restaurants, and night-spots.

The script tells us that *new and old* exist side by side so one should be placed slightly to the left and the other slightly to the right. Both should be referred to using the same pitch as they are equally desirable within the context of this script.

The *fashionable shopping areas, fine restaurants, and night-spots* each need to be 'placed' and kept at roughly the same pitch. If *night-spots* is delivered with a drop in pitch between the first and second half of the word it sounds less like somewhere you go to enjoy yourself and more like an undesirable facial eruption. Going down in the wrong place can completely change a meaning and cause a positive to become a negative. The tone of a voice-over can strongly influence the listener's feelings about what is being said and, since there are very few truly negative scripts, the tone must always be positive and optimistic.

Narration scripts can contain unfamiliar words and expressions – some of which look as if they ought to be easy to master and some of which look impossible. When delivering scripts with a highly technical, scientific, or medical content it is important to remember that your role is that of the informed speaker talking to an informed listener. The terminology used is familiar to both parties and difficult words and phrases should not be delivered with the showmanship of a conjurer performing a particularly skilful trick.

Campylobacter pylori bacillae should be no more dramatic than *Large red tomatoes*. A sentence as technically descriptive as: *The shoe houses the extrusion tool which comprises an entry block, die abutment, and an extrusion die* should sound simple, with the last three items being given a very strong sense of 'place'.

The voice-over artist is not expected to be familiar with terms such as the above, and scripts containing such difficult language are usually seen well in advance of the recording session. If you are sent a script in advance do not open the envelope for the first time in the studio. Not opening it until the day of the session displays both discourtesy and unprofessionalism – even if you know that the script contains only ten words of three letters each.

Scripts being recorded for medical use nearly always have an expert in the studio whose job it is to ensure that both pronunciation and 'sense' are absolutely accurate and clear.

Scripts containing foreign words pose particular problems. In everyday English English (as opposed to American English) the most common foreign words and sayings are usually French. While we pronounce *rendez-vous* and *fait accompli* in roughly the French style, we continue to love Paris, rather than *Paree* in the springtime. The solution is to pronounce foreign words in the way that they are heard in everyday speech and not to attempt the native pronunciation. One would not, for example, read a script about Scotland and turn on a fake Scottish accent for all place names.

Names and place names present the biggest problems, not because they are necessarily difficult but because their pronunciations are entirely idiosyncratic and do not follow rules. There is know way of knowing that the name 'Fetherstonehaugh' is pronounced 'Fanshaw' or that 'Belvoir' is 'Beever'. Equally, you need to be told that 'Wymondham' is 'Windam' and that 'Costessey' is 'Cossy'! In difficult cases it is possible to consult the Pronunciation Unit at the BBC in London. They specialise in advising the media on the correct pronunciation of names and place names world-wide, although this is not a free service.

4

Commercial Scripts

Commercial scripts vary a great deal in both content and quality. Most scripts for the advertising campaigns of international brand names are superbly crafted and give the voice artist the opportunity to create a perfectly timed and beautifully inflected delivery. Others are not so well written and give the unfortunate voice artist nothing more exciting than a headache. It is often the case that the poorly paid jobs involve the most difficult scripts. The problems lie in bad writing, poor command of language, and a desire to say as much as possible in the shortest available time. These scripts tend to fall into one of a number of easily identified clichés – the 'hard sell' furniture commercial is much the same throughout the world, while the sexy tone used to sell chocolate or ice-cream is instantly recognisable in most cultures. The skill lies in identifying which particular cliché is required and then delivering the script in a style which sounds fresh, new, and interesting! The secret is to be 100 per cent committed to the message, to make every word as meaningful as possible, and to enter into the 'world' of each particular script.

This chapter contains 15 scripts covering a wide range of styles of delivery. They were all written as either radio or TV commercials. Each one is analysed in detail, showing how the professional approaches the job of 'voicing' them. With experience this analysis becomes second nature and one does not consciously need to ask the 'who, how, what, when, where and why' questions.

I have given very precise instructions for the use of the three Ps – pitch, pace and pause. If you follow these instructions you will achieve a very professional 'read' and will have an understanding of the way in which different moods and emotions are created. However, all scripts are open to individual interpretation and much can be gained by experimenting and improvising. The Bombay Sapphire script can be delivered in the style of the Summit Furniture character and the Twinings Tea voice could be applied to the Rap and Hardcore Collection! These 'experiments' can be a very useful way of exploring a new or difficult script – just don't let the client hear you doing it. They might think you are satirising their beloved product!

Try all the scripts in this chapter as it is important to know your strengths and weaknesses. The discovery that your 'hard sell' is rather limp might save you from the ignominy of making a bad impression at an important audition. Word travels fast in the voice world, especially when it concerns an embarrassment or disaster.

When you have studied the analysis of each script you will find it easier to try it yourself working from a photocopy. You can experiment with 'marking up' the photocopy to remind you of pauses, phrase marks, upward inflections and 'turns'. The backing tracks are on the CD so scripts can be practised with the relevant music or FX; you could even use them to make your own voice tape.

BOMBAY SAPPHIRE – SOFT SELL

This is an extremely well-written script for an upmarket and internationally known brand. It occupies a 30-second slot and could feature a male or female voice. A suitable music and effects (M & E) track is on the CD. This script is for both radio and television.

> *It's pretty simple really*
> *Either you want to drink the best gin*
> *Or you don't.*
> *Bombay Sapphire*
> *Gin*
> *Only better.*

This script is open to many interpretations and characterisations. The 'voice' could be anything from an Australian builder's labourer to an upper class English society hostess. The important questions to ask about this script are: who and where; closely followed by: what am I really saying?

The following is one interpretation which casts a woman as the speaker, but it works equally well with both the sexes and roles reversed.

Who and Where?
You are a 30-year-old woman, wearing a black cocktail dress with all the appropriate accessories. You have taken time and trouble to get your appearance just the way you want it. You are in an expensive cocktail bar in an expensive hotel. The bar is fairly busy, and over in the corner a pianist is playing relaxed modern jazz.

You are sitting with your back to the bar so that you can see who comes in for a drink. Your body language makes it clear that you are prepared to be approached. An unaccompanied man comes into the room and stands next to you at the bar – a little closer to you than normal. He smiles at you and asks, by way of invitation, 'What are you drinking?' Your reply consists of the words of the script.

What am I saying?
It is important to realise that the one thing you are not talking about is gin! The script is in the form of a sexual invitation and the words are laden with ambiguity and innuendo.

When am I saying it?
This scene is definitely taking place in the evening.

When is it going to be broadcast/transmitted?
Because of the nature of the script and because it is an alcoholic product, this commercial is likely to be transmitted in the evenings. Consequently, a more 'adult' approach is appropriate.

Why am I saying it?
You are in search of a partner either for the evening or for life.

How am I saying it?
As there are only 20 words and the commercial spot is 30 seconds, the words must be spoken quite slowly. They are in the form of an intimate invitation between two people in a public place so they would probably be said quite discretely. The script is recorded as close to the microphone as possible, consistent with there being no 'pops' or mouth noises. This commercial demands superb vocal technique.

It's pretty simple really

This has to be alluring, making it very clear that there is a hidden agenda. It works best if delivered while smiling and slightly nodding the head. There should be slight pauses after *It's* and *really*. These create tension and heighten the interest of the listener. There should be an upward pitch movement within the word *really* to reinforce the sense of invitation. This can most easily be achieved by broadening the smile and raising the eyebrows.

Either you want to drink the best gin

This line breaks into two halves with a significant pause after *want*. The first half of the line leads the listener astray – of course he or she wants! The second half increases the tension by disguising the object of desire by referring to it as gin. It is very important to ensure that the two consecutive 't's in *want to* are sounded. They are sexually charged, and missing the first one destroys the atmosphere and sounds as if you are merely counting – *either you wan to*!

Or you don't.

This is a fine example of the positive negative. If it is delivered with a descending pitch pattern the script grinds to a halt on a negative note. The speaker is completely confident of the attractions of the product or service on offer and so a refusal would in no way dent his or her ego. The refusal would reflect badly on the person being tempted as they would clearly be considered incapable of rising to the occasion. This line has to be delivered with an even broader smile and an upward inflection on *don't*.

Bombay Sapphire

This is the only time the product is mentioned in the script and so these are the two most important words. They have to have the allure of the most exquisite sensual pleasure. The second half of *Sapphire* has to have an upward inflection. Many people find this very hard to achieve. If you treat it as a question in which you offer someone a choice between two brands of gin, the rise in pitch is too great to be suggestive – but it does get the voice moving in the right direction. The way to get the inflection absolutely right is to use the substitution technique described in chapter 3.

Gin

This innocently diffuses the suggestiveness of the previous line by implying '*Gin – what did you think I was talking about, you naughty person?*' This is achieved by using three distinct pitches within the one word. It is a hard technique to master if it does not happen naturally. It appears to have its roots in the early church music known as plainsong. The pitches used are the same as are used in the cadence which concludes some 'sung' psalms and prayers. It can therefore be learnt musically. The notes are A, F# and G, or any notes that give the same intervals – starting note, down three semitones, then up one semitone – for example, C, A and Bb. The word *gin* can be sung using these intervals so that you sound like a comic clergyman. The three notes slide effortlessly from one to the other with no breaks in-between.

Having practised the intervals, speed the process up so that the three notes occur in no more time than it would take to say the word normally. This is sometimes referred to as putting a 'turn' in the voice – a musical term used when an instrumentalist or singer

It's pretty simple really.
Either you want to drink the best Gin.....
Or you don't.
Bombay Sapphire
Gin.. only better.

A marked script – the upward arrows indicate rising inflections and the oblique strokes represent pauses. Notice how the word 'sex' has been written next to 'Gin' and 'bigger' has been pencilled in underneath 'better'.

decorates a particular note by quickly preceding it by both the note above and the note below. It is extremely important to master this technique and to be able to apply it without having to stop and think. It can be used to make a short and boring word a lot more interesting than it really is. It is something that we do in everyday speech but it can be very hard to contrive it when reading a script in front of a microphone.

The overall pitch of *gin* should be higher than that of *Bombay Sapphire*.

Only better.

Having misled and teased the listener the script now settles firmly for one option. This line must be delivered with all the allure and confidence of a person absolutely convinced of the quality and excitement of what they are offering. The word *Only* should be said quite slowly, with a teasing pause after it, and *better* should have an upward inflection and be delivered through a broadening smile. If this presents problems, the answer, once more, is to find a substitution that creates the desired effect and then change back to the original words. Both men and women may find the pitch pattern required by substituting *Only better* with *Only bigger*!

VIKING DIRECT – Hard Sell

This commercial occupies a 30 second slot and is for a large, successful company selling office supplies. They pride themselves on fast delivery, outstanding customer service, and highly competitive prices. The voice could be male or female. A music backing track for this radio commercial is on the CD.

It's the Price Buster Sale at Viking Direct, with all your
favourite office supplies at incredible prices:
Premium quality copier paper from 1.99 a ream,
Clear plastic folders – 3.49 for a hundred,
Boxes of Scotch sealing tape for £11.30,
And Bic highlighter pens an amazing 1.80 for a box of 5.
With free next-day delivery for any orders over £30
Viking Direct offers unbeatable value.
Call Viking – now – on Freephone 0800 42 44 44.

Bombay Sapphire was a very relaxed 20 words in 30 seconds, whereas *Viking Direct* is 77 words in exactly the same length of time. It is fast by any standards!

Who and Where?
The reader is a spokesperson for the company but not part of the company because there is no use of the first person plural – 'we'.

There is no 'where' – just a voice with an energetic musical accompaniment pushing it along.

What am I saying?
There is no hidden agenda; you are giving the good news about fantastic prices and free next-day delivery.

When am I saying it?
No specific time.

When is it going to be broadcast/transmitted?
It might be transmitted during the day to catch office supplies buyers listening to the radio at their desks, or it might be early morning or early evening to reach them on their way to or from work.

Why am I saying it?
You are excited by the good news and you want others to benefit from it.

How am I saying it?
It must be spoken quickly because of the word/time ratio of nearly three words per second and it must be with great enthusiasm. Your diction has to be perfect as every word carries important information. This is not the script for a bass voice. The ideal voice for this is fairly high pitched without being shrill or squeaky. This is not recorded close to the mic.

A commercial like this is not easy to get 'right' and some voice-over artists, knowing that such scripts are not one of their strengths, decline all invitations to perform them. They are very exciting to do and getting it 'right' creates a feeling of great satisfaction. Modern technology has made scripts like this very much easier to record as they do not now have to be completed in one take.

The first thing to do is to read it out loud for speed and diction. You need to know that the lips and tongue can cope with all the words and prices and the only way to do this is out loud – muttering in corners only perfects the non-productive skill of muttering in corners! Having established that there are no problems in delivering the script, the next job is to get it up to speed. It is a 30-second spot so the maximum time available for the script is 29½ seconds. Experienced voice-over artists 'know' the length of a 30-second commercial and can time it pretty accurately without a stopwatch. This script has to be 'punched out' to get the required energy. Concentrating on the energy will give you the required speed. The delivery has to be very physical with no loss of momentum at any point in the script.

The script has a 29½-second music bed to accompany it. It can be recorded with or without the music. My preference is always to work with the music as I think it helps the voice to flow from one end of the script to the other. Having music in the headphones (cans) gives you something to compete against so for scripts like this it helps to create a more energetic performance. After a few takes you get to know the structure of the music and it becomes a very helpful series of signposts against which you can judge your progress through the script – knowing whether to speed up, slow down, or keep going as you are.

Unfortunately, some engineers prefer you to work without the music in the cans. This may be because they are worried about spill between the mic and the cans – the mic picks up the sound of the music from your cans and it is recorded with your voice and cannot be removed at a later date. If the music is changed, or not used, there will still be slightly audible traces of it. However, if the engineer is doing his job properly and using the correct equipment this should not happen. Some engineers find it a little too much like hard work having to re-set and re-cue the music every time you go for another take. With modern multitrack recorders and computers it is easy to record the music on to the master recorder and replay it in parallel to the voice for every take. Computer systems will easily cope with two tracks of music (if it's in stereo) and 22 separate and different voice takes without causing the engineer any real inconvenience.

If you want to work with music you should be allowed to. Getting your own way in a studio without upsetting anyone is an important skill. Always remember that you are the one who has to deliver a performance – there are no excuses and no 'ifs' and 'buts'. The only thing that the public and your future employers want to hear is a perfect performance with no apologies or explanations. You have to do whatever it takes to achieve that.

The difficult thing about working with music is knowing when it is going to start. With a fast script it is vital to synchronise the start of the music with the start of the voice. The best way is to record a reverse count (5, 4, 3, 2, 1) on to the computer or recorder before the music so that both voice and music start on zero. This can be done either by the engineer or the voice artist. Some studios have a reverse count permanently available which they cut on to the front of each music bed as necessary. Hearing the reverse countdown gives you the time to prepare, to take and hold a breath, and to explode on to the first line.

It's the Price Buster Sale at Viking Direct,

This is the line that grabs the listener's attention so it is important to hit the first word quite hard. *Price Buster Sale* is the subject of the commercial so it needs to come across loud and clear, with *Sale* at a slightly higher pitch than the other words. This emphasises the word – volume cannot be used for emphasis in commercials as all words end up at roughly the same level. *Viking Direct* needs to be lifted because we want the listener to know, without doubt, *who* is having the sale. The whole script should be delivered slightly staccato with all words separated from each other – this gives a feeling of energy.

with all your favourite office supplies at incredible prices:

office supplies needs to be emphasised with a higher pitch so that we know what it is that is being sold. *Incredible prices* needs to be lifted because this is the teaser that keeps us listening.

Premium quality copier paper from 1.99 a ream,

I would record the above line and the next three lines separately as a series of drop-ins rather than attempting them all in one go. There are four specific and very interesting offers and it is important that each one of them has the same impact. If they are recorded in one go it is inevitable that the last two will be delivered with progressively less energy than the first two and there will be desperate intakes of breath between all of them. Recording them individually gives each the maximum impact and, if they can be made *not* to flow on from each other, they will have the same effect as if a salesman was leaping into vision from different sides of the picture before speaking the line.

All the words need to be emphasised, with the exception of *from* which can be shortened to 'frm'. The price is said as 'one ninety nine' rather than 'one pound ninety nine'. With a series of prices like these it is acceptable not to say 'pound' every time because it is clear what the prices are and there is no possibility of anyone being misled. To avoid misunderstandings, however, it is necessary at some point in any radio commercial to give a price using the word 'pound'. The plural 'pounds' is not used when there is a pence content to the price as it slightly impedes the flow. Television commercials can have the voice-over saying 'three ninety nine' for £3.99, or 'three ninety nine', 'three hundred and ninety nine', or 'three nine nine' for £399.00 – provided the price is displayed prominently on the screen.

Clear plastic folders – 3.49 for a hundred,

This line should be recorded as a drop-in with a slight upward inflection on *folders* followed by a minute suspense-building pause. *3.49 for a hundred* needs a feeling of joyful surprise; *3.49* is spoken as 'three forty nine'.

Boxes of Scotch sealing tape for £11.30,

Again, this is best recorded as a drop-in to get the renewed attack and enthusiasm. *Tape* definitely needs to be up in pitch, as if you are pointing to the product, and it should be followed by a slight pause. *For* should be shortened as much as possible and £11.30 should sound very enthusiastic. This price is read as 'eleven pounds thirty' because 'eleven thirty' sounds more like a time than a price!

And Bic highlighter pens an amazing 1.80 for a box of 5.

This line starts with an added value word designed to keep the listener's attention. We've given you premium quality copy paper, clear plastic folders, boxes of Scotch sealing tape, *and* if that wasn't enough to get you excited we are now going to hit you with Bic highlighter pens! *And* should have a lot of energy (not volume), should be said with a 'turn' in the voice (a movement in the pitch), and there must be a slight pause after it. *Bic highlighter pens* have to sound like the most exciting thing ever to hit an office desk, while *an amazing 1.80 for a box of 5* has to be just that – amazed!

With free next-day delivery for any orders over £30

This line should be done as a drop-in, paying particular attention to clarity of diction as it can be a tongue-twister. *Free* needs to be lifted in pitch to draw attention to it, as do *delivery, orders,* and *£30; £30* is said as 'thirty pounds' because 'thirty' would be meaningless.

Viking Direct offers unbeatable value.

This line must, of course, flow on from the previous one. It is only the second time that we hear the company name mentioned so it must be lifted. It is the second most important piece of information in the script. *Unbeatable value* has to be very positive.

Call Viking – now –

Call Viking needs to be an enthusiastic invitation rather than a command. *Now* must not sound like the barked command of a fierce Sergeant-Major. It is one of the most overused words in radio and television commercials and listeners are very resistant to it. However, advertisers (or their agency copywriters) love to use it and the voice-over artist has to find a way of making it work within the context of the script. One of the ways of dealing with it is to make it convey the idea that the advertiser is open for business at the very time you are hearing their commercial; *Now* means 'It's ten o'clock in the evening and we are here ready and waiting to take your order, please call us!' Advertisers using this invitation should ensure that their commercials are broadcast only during their opening hours.

on Freephone 0800 42 44 44.

This is the most important piece of information in the script. The listener might not be able to remember who the advertiser is or the precise details of their amazing sale prices, but they *must* remember the telephone number. *On Freephone* is the good news – it is not going to cost you anything to talk to them – so it must be cheerful. Smile when saying this. *0800* is a known Freephone prefix and should have a feeling of 'this bit's easy because you know this number already'. *42 44 44* is really all that has to be remembered. In chapter 3 I described the most memorable way of delivering it: 'forty two' has the highest pitch, 'forty four' is very slightly lower in pitch, the final 'forty' is lower still, and the final 'four' goes back up to the pitch of the initial number.

PANTENE HAIR SPRAY – Real Person Spot

This is a 40-second TV commercial for a world-famous brand of hair care product. It is one of a series featuring 'real' people in their 'real' place of work. It finishes with a 'tag' from a conventional voice-over. A female voice is used, with a male or female tag. A suitable music and effects backing track can be found on the CD.

> *As a journalist I'm on the go all day – so I need a hair spray I can rely on. I don't want to worry about how my hair looks. Styling used to make my hair look dull! Then I found Pantene.*
> *Pantene holds and protects your style on the outside while Pro-Vitamins nourish the hair on the inside. Whatever happens*

43

Pantene holds my hair the way I like it. So my hair looks really healthy and shiny – it never lets me down.
Pantene hair spray – great hold and healthy looking hair.

Who and Where?

You are a female journalist with a head of hair which you 'swish' from time to time. This coquettish activity is one of the memorable features of these commercials and this should have an impact on the 'real person' delivery. The Bombay Sapphire commercial is erotic – this one is flirtatious. You are just under 30 years old – but might have been so for a few years! You are in the busy newsroom of a national newspaper surrounded by journalists who are working at computers and making or taking phone calls. You are talking directly to us, and as you do so you move through the newsroom. The camera stays with you.

What am I saying?

You are telling us that Pantene hair spray performs two invaluable functions: not only does it hold your hair in whatever style you choose, but it simultaneously nourishes it on the inside with Pro-Vitamins. There is also the implication that if your hair looks and feels good you will have a more successful career.

When am I saying it?

Probably when newsrooms are at their busiest, which is in the afternoons and early evenings.

When is it going to be broadcast/transmitted?

Throughout the day and early evening.

Why am I saying it?

You are sharing one of the secrets of your success. If you look good you feel good. If you feel good you probably function more effectively both at work and play.

How am I saying it?

You are talking directly to camera and are talking only to us. Those around you cannot hear you and, apart from one particular moment, you have no direct interaction with them. You are confident in both your attractiveness and your abilities as a journalist. You need to be very secure in your characterisation – assuming a persona or accent which does not come naturally to you could make you 'non-believable'. It is important that the viewers are not distracted from the message by questioning the authenticity of the person delivering it. You are quite bright and bold. This is not recorded close to the mic.

As a journalist I'm on the go all day

The first thing you do is give us information about yourself – we know your profession and, because you are 'on the go all day', we know that you are successful. *Journalist* needs to be lifted, and *day* should have an upward inflection.

– so I need a hair spray I can rely on.

At this point you tell us the subject of the commercial. *Hair spray* needs to be lifted, and *I can rely on* should be said through a smile and end on an upward inflection.

I don't want to worry about how my hair looks.

A positive negative about which you have to sound cheerful; a downward inflection would interrupt the flow of information. The secret is to lift *looks* and not *hair*. We already know that we are talking about hair because *hair spray* was lifted in the previous line. If you did worry, which of course you don't, it would not be your hair but the *look* of it that gave you cause for concern.

Styling used to make my hair look dull!

Another positive negative. Deal with this by having an affectionate chuckle at the mistakes of the past, secure in the knowledge that everything is now sweetness and light. End on an up with an upward shrug of the shoulders.

Then I found Pantene.

Here comes the cavalry! *Then* should be treated as an added value word. It is not, but in this context a 'turn' in the pronunciation and a pause either side of it will serve to emphasise the name of the product. *Pantene* must be lifted and has to be given a sense of 'place' because you would either produce one out of your handbag or a can will appear on screen.

Pantene holds and protects your style on the outside

This line starts with a repeat of the product name which needs a different and slightly more enthusiastic inflection. It then goes on to tell us of one of the major benefits of the product. The *and* in this line should not be treated as an added value word. The sense is that 'holding and protecting' are combined as one. Two major benefits are being claimed for the product and they are both given equal importance. To achieve this, give them both a sense of 'place'. Point to *holds and protects your style on the outside* in a fixed upper position to the left of you.

while Pro-Vitamins nourish the hair on the inside.

Place this, the other major benefit, in an equal fixed upper position to the right of you. As in the Shakespearean device – on the one hand you have 'this' and on the other hand you have 'that' – so with Pantene you have *protects your style on the outside* balanced against *nourish the hair on the inside. Outside* and *inside* must have equal weight and position. In this statement we come across *Pro-Vitamins* for the first time. They imply an added ingredient which benefits the user so they must be lifted.

Whatever happens Pantene holds my hair the way I like it.

Here we have room for a little humour. This is the point at which the real person can interact with either her colleagues or her surroundings. There has to be a reason for saying *Whatever happens.* Something has to happen for her to react to. This is a script for a TV commercial – on screen an electric fan might have blown her hair out of place, or the office comedian might have launched a paper aeroplane at her. If you practise or record this script it is likely to be audio only so the trick is to visualise something happening and react to it by laughing through the line. Lift the product name and end on an upward inflection.

So my hair looks really healthy and shiny

This statement is both positive and happy; watch out for *really healthy and shiny.*

– it never lets me down.

Shake the head for the positive negative of *never*, but smile broadly to turn it into a positive. *Down* must be up!

Pantene hair spray – great hold and healthy looking hair.

This is a 'tag' – it can be the same female voice, a different female voice, or a male voice. It is recorded close to the mic to give a more intimate sound quality than has been used in the main body of the commercial. This should be delivered with a pattern of gradually ascending pitches – each word should be slightly higher than the one before it. Slowly raising a hand during the delivery will help to achieve this!

MAK CAR CARE CENTRES –
Comic Character Spot

This is a 30-second radio commercial with its own specially written jingle which concludes with female voices singing the advertiser's name and telephone number. This jingle can be found on the CD. A male or female voice can be used.

The script is based on research which suggests that women are not as familiar as men with the technical terms for car faults. Whereas a man might go to Service Reception and say, 'I think my tappets (valves) need adjusting', a woman is more likely to say 'There's a bonking under the bonnet'. A slack big-end refers to wear in the main bearings, and some Citroen cars have suspension systems which need the occasional repressurising – known as a pump-up. This commercial embraces a very 'English' humour, much in the style of the 'Carry On' films, and it is not intended to cause offence to delicate sensibilities of either a sexual or political persuasion. It is funny!

Ladies, is there a bonking under your bonnet?
Is your big-end slack?
Does your suspension need a pump-up?
Well, we don't care how you describe it
Pick up the phone
Call MAK Car Care Centres
We'll sort you out – no problem!
Sung Jingle: MAK Car Care Centres – 5 0 5 0 1

Who and Where?
The original version used a female voice, but it has subsequently been recorded by both male and female. You are the owner, the receptionist or a mechanic. As you say *We'll sort you out* you must be part of the company – not a spokesperson for it.

What am I saying?
You are acknowledging the fact that women are suspicious of garages because they suspect them of blinding them with technicalities and of overcharging. You are saying that MAK Car Care Centres are friendly and will listen to what you have to say about your car problems.

When am I saying it?
No specific time.

When is it going to be broadcast/transmitted?
Probably mornings and afternoons to catch housewives at home.

Why am I saying it?
You are persuading female customers that they should call your garage.

How am I saying it?
These are the particular challenges presented by this script: being entertaining, not being offensive, and getting through the spoken

script before the jingle – without sounding rushed or panicked. A female voice needs to be friendly and reassuring with a sense of humour. A male voice can be either a 'cheeky chappie' or a 'nerd'. He must not make the sexual innuendo threatening. One solution is for him to be camp! He can have almost any national or regional accent.

Ladies,

This is very specific and makes it clear who the commercial is aimed at. Use an upward inflection.

Is there a bonking under your bonnet?

The first three lines of the script would benefit from being recorded one at a time to stop them sounding as if they are coming from and going to exactly the same place. If a series of questions are recorded in one take, only the first of them has the necessary energy – the others sound as if they form part of an interrogation. All three should start at different pitches – the first high, the second low, and the third somewhere in between. If they are recorded separately and on different tracks of a multitrack computer or recorder they can be placed left, right and centre in the stereo picture, which makes for a more interesting sound. Recording multitrack allows them to be very slightly overlapped so that one question starts just as the previous one finishes. The stereo positioning and the overlapping trick the unsuspecting listener into believing that there is more than one person voicing the commercial.

Excellent diction is very important – *bonking* and *bonnet* need to be very clear, and the question needs to be just that – a question! Excellent diction, in this context, means pronouncing the word in such a way that what you are saying is absolutely clear. This is possible in any accent – from cockney to Brooklyn.

Is your big-end slack?

The second question. *Big-end* and *slack* must be very clear, with the 'd' and 'ck' sounded. This question can be said with a slight chuckle in the voice, or, if you have gone for the 'nerd' option, a nasal snort halfway through.

Does your suspension need a pump up?

All three questions can be characterised as three different people with different voices. This line can work particularly well with a French accent in the Pink Panther style of Peter Sellers! This is the cheekiest of the three questions and can be delivered with a broad smile to emphasise the sense of fun.

Well,

Having hooked your listener with entertaining voices and unusual questions you now start to get the sales message across. This word is the mid-point in the commercial. It is the 'turning point' between entertaining and selling. To diffuse any tension or ambiguity generated by the first half of the commercial, the word should be slightly elongated and given a downward inflection. At this point you might choose to revert to a more 'normal' voice.

we don't care how you describe it

Lift the pitch from the end of the previous word and use a slightly descending pitch pattern as far as *you*, then lift the pitch of *describe it*. The overall tone should be very friendly.

Pick up the phone

A very friendly instruction with an upward inflection.

Call

Isolate this word, pitch it higher than *phone*, and put a turn in it to make it interesting.

MAK Car Care Centres

MAK is pronounced as three separate letters – M A K. This is a tongue twister! The natural inclination is to give it a downward pitch pattern which is completely wrong. This is the first mention of the name of the advertiser and it has to be memorable. Inflect it as if it were the answer to the question – 'I've got a terrible problem with my car – who is going to help me?' The pitch should ascend, with *Car* having the highest pitch, and *Care* and *Centres* being pitched progressively lower. The pitch pattern should have the feel of ascending one side of an inverted semi-circle and descending the other. This pitch pattern and the four consecutive 'k' sounds combine to make this a very difficult phrase to get right. It might help to trace the shape of an inverted semi-circle in the air while delivering it.

We'll sort you out – no problem!

Very friendly, very reassuring. Best said through a smile with a large wink during *no problem*.

Timing is extremely important in this commercial. The jingle starts with two distinct isolated beats (known as the 'bonks') which are immediately followed by the word *Ladies*. The script then has to be finished by the time the jingle starts. To be talking when they start is known as 'crashing' the jingle and is one of the ultimate sins in voice-over. In this case the jingle contains vital information

Ladies is there a bonking under your bonnet?

Is your big end slack?

Does your suspension need a pump-up?

Well, we don't care how you describe it

Pick up the phone

Call MAK Car Care Centres

We'll sort you out - no problem.

> *'Yer' has been written over 'your' to remind the performer not to be too up-market in diction. The words 'no problem' have been pencilled alongside the last three lines to draw attention to the fact that the script creates anxiety and then offers solutions. The semi-circular mark over the penultimate line is a phrase mark indicating that 'MAK Car Care Centres' should be delivered as one smooth phrase.*

– the restatement of the name of the advertiser and the only mention of their phone number. If you finish the script two or three seconds before they start you are wasting selling time and the client will be unhappy. Start after the two bonks and finish half a second before the singing starts.

BT CALLMINDER – Informing and Selling

BT (formerly known as British Telecom) is one of the largest companies in the world. They operate mostly in the telecommunications business. This is a 45-second commercial for radio or television describing the benefits of a telephone message service. This is 'awareness' advertising – they are selling a product but they do not tell you how to get in touch with them in order to take advantage of it. A male or female voice can be used and there is a 45-second music backing track on the CD.

> *If the thought of returning home from a holiday or business trip to a deluge of messages doesn't appeal to you – BT Callminder should. BT Callminder is one of the most advanced systems around and offers some distinct advantages. To operate*

the system all you need is a tone dialling telephone or a pocket-sized keypad.

When you're out and someone wants to contact you they simply dial your normal telephone number and leave their message. Collecting it couldn't be easier! Just pick up the nearest phone – call your own number and enter your pin using a touchtone phone or keypad. Your messages can then be played back to you no matter where you are in the world.

BT – Stay in touch.

Who and Where?

It initially reads as if you are a spokesperson or an announcer, but the final line makes you part of the company. You are a BT employee and are probably in a BT showroom explaining the product to a potential purchaser. There is nothing physical to purchase as Callminder is a digital system to which you subscribe – the equipment remains in the telephone exchange and not in your home. The advantage is that you can collect your messages from any telephone anywhere in the world.

What am I saying?

You are telling us how easy the system is to use. You are flattering us by suggesting that we lead international jet-setting lives and need to be in constant touch with our base.

When am I saying it?

During normal business hours.

When is it going to be broadcast/transmitted?

Probably in the evenings to catch small businessmen relaxing in hotel bedrooms.

Why am I saying it?

This is awareness advertising and is usually only undertaken by very large international corporations who have no real need to advertise because they either have a monopoly or they are a household name. You are telling us about yet another fantastic service from BT which only serves to justify their position as a world leader.

How am I saying it?

Very quietly and confidently, but light and friendly. You have to make it sound a very easy system to use as some people suffer from techno-phobia. There is a very friendly tag.

If the thought of returning home from a holiday or business trip

The first word needs to be hit quite hard – it acts as a springboard to get the script off to a good start. Lift *home*, and place *holiday* to the left and *business trip* to the right. This separates them as activities but also gives them equal weight.

to a deluge of messages

A positive negative. Getting a deluge of messages can be a nuisance (the negative), but it shows either that you are important or that people care about you (the positive). Say it with a smile! *Deluge* is one of those foreign words mentioned earlier. The pronunciation should not be French.

doesn't appeal to you

Yet again a positive negative. It is positive because we are about to offer an alternative, so this negative is an essential part of the proceedings and should be welcomed. Emphasise *doesn't* and place it on one side because it will soon be offset and balanced by *should*.

– BT Callminder should!

This is the first mention of the company and their product so lift both words and put a turn in *Callminder*. Place the product on the opposite side to the *deluge of messages* and make sure that *should* is lifted even further.

BT Callminder is one of the most advanced systems around

The name of the product is repeated so a slightly different inflection is called for. The first of the customer benefits is mentioned and this needs an upward inflection.

and offers some distinct advantages.

Another customer benefit and another upward inflection on *distinct advantages.*

To operate the system

This introduces some semi-technical information so the speed of the delivery should slow up a little.

all you need is a tone dialling telephone

Lift *tone dialling telephone* slightly and place it (the telephone) to one side.

or a pocket sized keypad.

Make it sound like the most everyday object in the world; give it the same pitch as the telephone and place it on the other side. This is the halfway point of the script and should have taken 22 seconds.

When you're out

Flatter the listener – they're busy! Slow up a little more and keep the inflection up.

and someone wants to contact you

More flattery – they may be busy but people still need to contact them. The emphasis is on *contact* not *you*.

they simply dial your normal telephone number

Make this instruction sound simple and light – the emphasis is on *dial* but should not be too heavy. Keep the inflection up at the end.

and leave their message.

It must have the feeling that 'nothing could be simpler'. Again keep the inflection up at the end.

Collecting it couldn't be easier!

This can be said through a reassuring, friendly smile. You are now about to ask the listener to do something so slow up a little.

Just pick up the nearest phone

Make it sound very simple without being condescending. Point to the nearest phone to give the script a feeling of reality.

call your own number

Keep the tone up and make dialling movements.

and enter your pin

Slow up a little more and make sure the diction is perfect – this is the hardest part of the instructions.

using a touchtone phone or keypad.

Point to the phone and keypad that you earlier placed to your left and right.

Your messages can then be played back to you

Relax a little, lift *messages* and *back to you.*

no matter where you are in the world!

Relax and smile. This is flattery. We know the listener is probably in some non-descript industrial city but we are pretending that they are in Hawaii! There is an element of selling dreams and lifestyles.

BT – Stay in touch.

Very warm and friendly with a smile and wink on *Stay in touch.*

This is not an easy script to do well and it is usually recorded in sections rather than in one long take. I suggest a lot of upward inflections, but ideally these should only be slight increases in pitch. When trying this, the beginner often finds that their whole voice pitch shifts up alarmingly and they sound very shrill. This is perfectly normal and it needs a conscious effort to keep the overall pitch low with only slight lifts. What the beginner forgets is that an upward inflection only works if you go down again immediately after it. An upward inflection should only stick its head slightly above the parapet of the average pitch. It must not be as extreme as the Australian rising inflection.

TWININGS TEA – Character Spot

Twinings are probably the best-known growers and blenders of English tea. Their brand is world-famous. This is a 40-second radio commercial adapted from their magazine advertising. The voice can be either male or female, and the music and effects backing track is on the CD.

> *For those of you who aren't at their best in the mornings – our English Breakfast Tea always delivers a bright, full bodied flavour, a brisk blend of Indian and Ceylon leaf that's strong enough to lift the most jaded spirit.*
>
> *Not surprisingly lots of people rely on it for their first cup of the day.*
>
> *Twinings – one of the nicer things to do in the morning.*

Who and Where?
The M & E track starts with the sound of two people snoring rather unpleasantly, an alarm clock rings, and they begin to wake up amidst much groaning and spluttering. You appear in their 'morning after the night before' bedroom. They are unable to see you. You are immaculately dressed, you have been awake for hours, and you are holding a beautiful cup and saucer containing a freshly brewed cup of Twinings English Breakfast Tea. You are a good old-fashioned English snob. You clearly disapprove of the surroundings in which you find yourself and the dreadful people who inhabit them. If you are male you can play this script as a butler in the style of the P. G. Wodehouse character 'Jeeves'. If you are female you can be a very upper class 'county' lady.

What am I saying?
You are saying that people with 'standards' drink Twinings English Breakfast Tea. It is a reviving beverage and drinking it is often

considered a preferable activity to anything else that two people might get up to in bed in the morning! There is the grudging acknowledgement that other companies might produce an English Breakfast Tea, however, *ours* is infinitely superior. It is a drink which is eminently suitable for people with both taste and standards.

When am I saying it?
Early morning.

When is it going to be broadcast/transmitted?
Mornings and evenings.

Why am I saying it?
You want to convert us to the brand and introduce the catch-phrases: *For those of you who aren't at their best in the mornings* and *Twinings – one of the nicer things to do in the morning*. The expectation is that people will replay the scene in their own bedrooms while bringing their partner a cup of Twinings Tea.

How am I saying it?
In a very haughty and superior tone of voice. The delivery should be quite relaxed and with large jumps in pitch.

For those of you who aren't at their best in the mornings

This script requires immaculate diction throughout. The whole thing can be preceded by an obvious and disapproving intake of breath. *Aren't* needs to be isolated by pauses and slightly lifted in pitch. *Mornings* needs an upward inflection.

Our English Breakfast Tea

Other companies make English Breakfast Tea but we need to emphasise *our*. The two consecutive Ts – *Breakfast Tea* – must be sounded. *English Breakfast Tea* is the name of the product and the three words need to have a feeling of cohesiveness. The most effective way to achieve this is to give them all the same pitch.

always delivers a bright, full bodied flavour,

Imagine that you are holding a delicious cup of tea and *bright, full bodied flavour* is an appreciative reaction to the enticing aroma. Keep the pitch up at the end.

a brisk blend of Indian and Ceylon leaf

Another reaction to the quality of the product. The *and* is not an added value word in this context and so does not need to be emphasised. *Leaf* must be lifted so that the next line flows on from this.

that's strong enough to lift the most jaded spirit.

Keep the pitch up as far as *most*, follow it with a slight pause and then drop the pitch as far as possible in an obvious and disapproving reference to the two inhabitants of the room.

Not surprisingly

Return to the normal pitch and deliver the words with a very haughty tone – emphasise the 't' of *not*.

lots of people rely on it

Continue with the perfect diction – closing the eyes for *rely on it* helps produce an even more haughty tone.

for their first cup of the day.

Soften and become a little warmer on *first cup of the day.*

Twinings

Maintain the character but deliver this word with a warm, superior smile.

One of the nicer things to do in the morning.

Slightly isolate *nicer* as a reference to what the couple in the room might, or might not, have been up to, and as a further reference to the euphemistic use of the brand name.

CRISIS – Real Person Spot

This is a 60-second radio commercial for a major English charity which specialises in providing food, care and shelter for homeless people at Christmas time. This is known as a 'Direct Appeal'. The charity pays for the airtime and production costs. The commercial is broadcast at the beginning of a commercial break and a 10-second tail is broadcast at the end of the same break. It can be spoken by either a male or a female voice. It is a real 'real person' spot and should not be contrived.

Hello, my name's ...

I don't know what you're doing this Christmas, but in just a few days I'll be part of an enormous operation to put a smile on the face of London's homeless people. I'm a volunteer for the Crisis Open Christmas.

Right now Crisis is equipping Olympia Exhibition Centre with mattresses, blankets and cooking and washing facilities to house London's homeless people over the Christmas period.

Alongside me, over 2,000 people will be giving up their

time to help run shelters like these. Doctors have volunteered. And hairdressers. And chiropodists.

This is part of a country-wide operation to give homeless people a few days' shelter from the freezing winter nights. And it's a chance for Crisis to help homeless people start to put their lives back together.

It's too late for you to volunteer this year. But you can still help. Please call Freephone 08000 38 48 38 with your credit card. £25 could help pay for food or heating. That's 08000 38 48 38. Thank you.

Ten second tail broadcast at end of commercial break:

Please help Crisis give homeless people a happy Christmas. Call 08000 38 48 38 with your credit card. Thank you.

Who and Where?
You are one of the volunteers and are in a studio recording this commercial. There is no M & E track to accompany the recording.

What am I saying?
Many people intend to volunteer to help Crisis at Christmas time but they usually leave it too late to volunteer. You are telling people that it *is* now too late to volunteer but if they still want to help the thing needed most is money. Credit card donations are being accepted. There is an implied reminder to volunteer in good time for next Christmas.

When am I saying it?
No specific time.

When is it going to be broadcast/transmitted?
During the day in December – to catch people with time on their hands and credit cards in their pockets.

Why am I saying it?
To raise money and to keep the name of the charity in the public domain.

How am I saying it?
Absolutely straight with no contrivances.

Hello, my name's ...

Fill in your own name, or, if you find it difficult to talk about yourself, use a different one.

I don't know what you're doing this Christmas, but

An accurate statement but with the feel of a question.

in just a few days

This is not important information.

I'll be part of an enormous operation to put a smile on the face of London's homeless people.

A slight pause after *operation* helps to draw attention to what follows. In the UK the words *homeless people* are run together to form one noun, with the stress being placed on the adjective *homeless* rather than the noun *people*. If the two words are separated and *people* is given a slightly higher pitch it becomes much more powerful. The homeless are first and foremost *people*.

I'm a volunteer for the Crisis Open Christmas.

A simple statement of fact. Make sure that *Crisis Open Christmas* comes across clearly as it is the first mention of the charity.

Right now Crisis is equipping Olympia Exhibition Centre with mattresses, blankets and cooking and washing facilities to house London's homeless people over the Christmas period.

Make sure that *Olympia Exhibition Centre* comes across clearly. Lift *people* and *Christmas period*.

Alongside me, over 2,000 people will be giving up their time to help run shelters like these.

Put the emphasis on *me*, *help*, and *these*.

Doctors have volunteered. And hairdressers. And chiropodists.

Simple statements – lift each of the three professions.

This is part of a country-wide operation to give homeless people a few days' shelter from the freezing winter nights.

Run the words *country-wide operation* together and give each the same pitch – do not fall into the trap of going down. Lift *people*, *shelter*, and *nights*.

And it's a chance for Crisis to help homeless people start to put their lives back together.

Lift *chance* and separate *people* from *homeless*.

It's too late for you to volunteer this year. But you can still help.

Lift *year* and *help*.

58

Please call Freephone 08000 38 48 38 with your credit card.

The telephone number is all important as it is the only point of contact given so it has to be made easy to memorise. Lift *Freephone* and *08000*, which is said as 'oh eight thousand'. *38* should be up, *48* down, and *38* back up to the initial pitch; it is said as 'thirty eight, forty eight, thirty eight'. Lift *credit card.*

£25 could help pay for food or heating.

This is said as 'twenty five pounds'. Lift the word *pounds* and put a turn in it. Lift and place *food* and *heating.*

That's 08000 38 48 38. Thank you.

Leave a slight pause after *that's* then repeat the phone number as before. *Thank you* should be simple, not too over the top, perhaps with a slight downward inflection.

Ten-second tail broadcast at end of commercial break

Please help Crisis give homeless people a happy Christmas. Call 08000 38 48 38 with your credit card. Thank you.

The emphasis should be on *please*, with *help* being at a lower pitch. *Crisis* is slightly lifted. In this context *homeless people* can be run together. *Christmas* should be very slightly higher in pitch than *Happy*. The rest of the tail is as before.

BLACK GOLD – Soft Sexy Sell

Black Gold is a world-famous brand of coffee from Nescafé. The script takes place within 10-seconds. A male or a female voice could be used. This copy is used on both radio and television, and may be the tag to a longer commercial.

> *New*
> *Black Gold*
> *From Nescafé.*
> *A rich revelation in taste.*

Who and Where?
You are a disembodied studio voice-over delivering this as a complete commercial or as a tag. You are sexy – males need to have a very dark brown chocolatey voice; women need to sound seductive.

What am I saying?
You are suggesting that Nescafé Black Gold is a sexy product.

When am I saying it?
Late at night.

When is it going to be broadcast/transmitted?
Evenings and late at night.

Why am I saying it?
You want the brand to be associated with enjoyable pastimes – you are inviting people to try it for themselves, just to see what it is like.

How am I saying it?
Very quietly, very close to the mic, and very sexily.

New

This needs to be breathed into the mic with a downward inflection. It should not be whispered – there should be plenty of 'chest' in the voice.

Black Gold

Be sure to sound the 'ck' of *Black*. Pitch *Gold* just a little higher with a suggestive turn in the voice. This can be achieved by raising an eyebrow.

From Nescafé.

The *from* can be quite short with a pause after it. *Nescafé* needs a suggestive upward inflection between *Nes* and *café*. The fact that it is from *Nescafé* makes everything all right.

A rich revelation

Take your time over this and nod appreciatively during *revelation*.

in taste.

Leave a suggestive pause after *in* and deliver *taste* as if you might be doing something quite unexpected (but interesting) with the coffee granules.

SKY DIGITAL TELEVISION – A Two-hander

This is a 40-second television commercial which also features a child's voice. The original music used in the commercial is on the CD and the two lines spoken by the child are pre-recorded on top of it in the correct places. The voice used can be either male or female.

Child: *I want the newest episodes of my favourite programmes.*

Only Sky Digital has the widest choice of quality TV channels and movies starting at times to suit you.

Child: *I want news, and music, and sport.*

All in crystal clear digital picture and sound from only £6.99 a month.
Visit your sky retailer or call 08702 42 42 42.
Let's talk about what you want, right now.
Sky Digital.

Who and Where?
You are part of Sky because you say '*let's*', which is, of course, short for let *us*. You are an unashamed studio voice-over.

What am I saying?
You are telling the viewer how good it is and how cheap it is.

When am I saying it?
No specific time.

When is it going to be broadcast/transmitted?
At all times, but not, for obvious reasons, on Sky Television.

Why am I saying it?
You want the viewer to stop watching the commercial channel they are tuned to and take out a subscription to Sky Digital.

How am I saying it?
In a warm and friendly tone. The music is relaxed and dreamlike so the voice is not at all 'pushy'.

Only Sky Digital

The child's first line is on the CD so you have to follow her. Slightly emphasise *Only* and lift *Sky Digital* because it is the product name.

has the widest choice of quality TV channels and movies

This all needs to be lifted slightly. The *and* is not an added value word.

starting at times to suit you.

The 't' in *at* can be lost because sounding it before *times* would feel a little contrived and would break the flow. Lift *you* and point to an imaginary viewer so that the listener really feels it is a service

61

designed to benefit them alone. This section has to be timed to fit exactly before the child's second line, with a natural sounding gap between the two.

All in crystal clear digital picture and sound from only £6.99 a month.

This starts after the child's second line. It should be one phrase as far as *sound*, with a slight feeling of waxing lyrical. Pause after *sound* and smile during the price information; it is said as 'six pound ninety nine'.

Visit your Sky retailer

Lift *retailer*.

or call 08702 42 42 42.

Pause after *call*, then the number is said as 'oh eight seven oh two'. All the numbers are spoken at the same pitch, but 2 is lifted slightly and given a turn to make it interesting. The rest of the number is 'forty two, forty two, forty two', again all at the same pitch but with raised eyebrows on the last forty two.

Let's talk about what you want, right now.

This is very warm and friendly – make sure the *you* refers to one specific person and not to a group of people.

Sky Digital.

Said with warmth and a smile.

SUMMIT FURNITURE – A Comic Character Spot

This is a 30-second radio spot using either a male or female voice. There is a specially composed jingle which bears a very slight resemblance to the theme from a well-known British television series chronicling the misfortunes of some less than competent petty criminals. The singing girls appear at the end of the jingle giving us the name of the store and their sales catchphrase.

> *'Ere, you listening? There's this lorry load of something rather tasty just arrived at Summit Furniture, Wood Green. It wasn't delivered – it fell off the back of a lorry, a Danish lorry. Know what I mean? It's got to be sold fast! Cash or interest-free credit – written credit details on request. You'll love it! Remember – Summit Furniture, Wood Green. Nip in quick 'fore it's all gone.*

Who and Where?
You are a comic criminal and you have accosted us on a street corner in an attempt to sell us some furniture of dubious origin.

What am I saying?
That Summit Furniture are selling off some furniture quickly and cheaply and it might not be wise to question its provenance. This is the chance to get a 'no questions asked' bargain. It is, of course, a comic fantasy because the store in question would never sell anything that had not been obtained through the normal channels of supply.

When am I saying it?
No specific time.

When is it going to be broadcast/transmitted?
At all times, but probably quite intensively until the sale is over.

Why am I saying it?
The shop wants to clear out some stock quite quickly.

How am I saying it?
This is a moderately fast read. There is one bar of music before you start and the whole thing has to be completed before the closing jingle. You have to create the character of a friendly villain. He would be talking quite quietly so that he is not overheard by the 'wrong' people. This kind of comically villainous script is best delivered while standing on the balls of the feet – as if ready to make a quick exit if the law arrives. These characters use a lot of hand and head movements when talking, and they are always looking around to see what else might, or might not, be going on. This constant jerky movement results in a rather idiosyncratic delivery. Only attempt this kind of script if you are confident of your characterisation. The Dick Van Dyke school of loveable cockneys is no longer popular with advertisers!

'Ere, you listening?

The script starts after the first bar of music at the same point as the drums start playing. It may be necessary to listen to the track on the CD a few times to become familiar with it. If you were doing the job for real the track would be played to you a few times before you started recording. The opening line should be said as an urgent throaty whisper, close to the mic, and probably delivered out of the side of the mouth. It is not actually whispered – this would only work if the whole script was whispered. It has to have the *feeling* of a whisper.

There's this lorry load of something rather tasty

Put a slight pause before *rather tasty* and elongate the 'a' in *rather*. *Tasty* should be lifted in pitch.

just arrived at Summit Furniture, Wood Green.

Make sure that *Summit Furniture* and *Wood Green* are slightly isolated and lifted in pitch to make it very clear who is advertising and where they are to be found.

It wasn't delivered

A positive negative. Shake the head, smile, and raise the eyebrows while saying it. *Delivered* should have the highest pitch.

it fell off the back of a lorry,

This is a euphemism for having been obtained other than by the normal rules of trade. It is said with wide-eyed innocence and a chuckle.

a Danish lorry. Know what I mean?

Which tells us that it must be highly desirable Scandinavian furniture, so lift *Danish. Know what I mean?* This is a throw-away phrase much beloved of cockney characters. The words are run together, the middle 't' is lost – 'Nowhaeyemeen?' – and the whole thing is posed as a question.

It's got to be sold fast!

Back to the serious business. Deliver the line out of the side of the mouth with a pause after *sold* to emphasise the higher pitched *fast*.

Cash or interest-free credit –

This character usually prefers *cash*, but in this case he also likes *interest-free credit*. Keep the pitch rising so *credit* is the highest point.

written credit details on request.

And then the pitch drops and this line is thrown away (in character) because these words are a legal necessity in the UK and do not sell anything.

You'll love it!

Renewed enthusiasm!

Remember – Summit Furniture, Wood Green.

Use an ascending pitch throughout this line. This is a repeat of the most important information – as long as the listener knows 'who' and 'where', the 'what' will be there for them when they arrive.

Nip in quick 'fore it's all gone.

Best delivered quickly while moving or turning away from the mic to give the impression of a rapid departure. This line must not crash the jingle which restates the store's name.

HOSEASONS HOLIDAYS – Soft, non-sexy sell

This is a 30-second radio and television commercial aimed at families. Hoseasons is an old, established English family firm providing holiday destinations throughout the UK and continental Europe. The holiday sound effects track is on the CD. A male or female voice can be used.

> *There's more holiday choice from Hoseasons. Over fifty years of holiday experience goes into giving you an ever growing choice of holiday ideas.*
> *Ring us now for the brochure of your choice.*
> *For delightful cottages in the British countryside call 01 502 502 603*
> *For relaxing boating holidays in France and Belgium call 01 502 502 604*
> *And for continental holiday parks in Germany, Holland, and Belgium call 01 502 502 605.*
> *There's more holiday choice from Hoseasons.*

Who and Where?
You are a fresh and fit young mum or dad, probably in your thirties, and blessed with 2.4 well-behaved, happy children. You appear in the three different locations mentioned.

What am I saying?
You are saying that Hoseasons is a reputable company that takes the worry out of booking a holiday and offers relaxing family activities.

When am I saying it?
On holiday in the summer.

When is it going to be broadcast/transmitted?
Saturation coverage all day over the Christmas and New Year break, then regularly until Easter. Mostly early morning and early evening.

Why am I saying it?
To get people to request brochures and thereby build up a 'holiday specific' mailing list.

How am I saying it?

You are very relaxed, calm, and very smiley. There is no hint of the usual problems and arguments that accompany family holidays.

There's more holiday choice from Hoseasons.

Said with a big smile. Lift and isolate *more holiday choice*, shorten *from* to 'frm', and place *Hoseasons* as if you were pointing to it on a nameboard. It is pronounced 'Hoeseasons'.

Over fifty years of holiday experience goes into giving you an ever growing choice of holiday ideas.

Still smiling, the words *holiday experience* are slightly run together. *Giving you* is not *giving you* – the stress is on the 'g' of *giving*. Pause slightly after *choice*, and then lift *holiday ideas*.

Ring us now for the brochure of your choice.

Keep this as a friendly invitation rather than an instruction. Isolate *now* by putting a pause either side of it. Slightly emphasise (with pitch not volume) *brochure* and give an upward inflection to *choice*.

For delightful cottages in the British countryside

This is the first of three categories and it should be clear to the listener that others will follow. Keep *countryside* up and give the kind of turn which conveys the message: 'there are more to come'. Smile.

call 01 502 502 603

Do not emphasise *call* as there are two more destinations and numbers to come. The number is 'oh one, five oh two, five oh two – six oh three' with the final three being lifted to convey the message that there are others to come. It can help to give the number a place and point to it as if written on a poster.

For relaxing boating holidays in France and Belgium call 01 502 502 604

Lift *boating holidays* and make sure that *France and Belgium* really are different places. The telephone number is the same but lift the 'four' so that we know there is more to come.

And for continental holiday parks in Germany, Holland, and Belgium call 01 502 502 605.

This is an added value *and* so isolate it. Lift *continental holiday parks* and point to *Germany, Holland, and Belgium*. The number is spoken in exactly the same way as the previous two, but inflect the 'five' in such a way that we know the numbers have finished.

This can be done by saying it with outstretched arms and upward facing palms or, if all else fails, by giving it a downward inflection.

There's more holiday choice from Hoseasons.

Give a big warm smile, a slight pause after *choice*, and a lift for *Hoseasons*.

RAP AND HARDCORE COLLECTION – Hard 'Street' Sell

This is a 20-second radio commercial for either a male or female voice. It is aimed at 'young people' – anyone who would be interested in buying and listening to this collection of club tracks. It is hard hitting, aggressive, loud, up-front, in-yer-face, and definitely not a sales pitch. That's how it has to appear to be but, like all things contrived not to sound contrived, it follows the same basic principles as every other commercial. The contrivances have to be well disguised in order not to alienate the target audience. The 20-second backing track is on the CD.

> *It's the Greatest Rap & Hardcore Collection ever!!*
> *65 Rap & Hardcore originals featuring:*
> *Dina Carroll*
> *Simon Harris*
> *Heavy D*
> *Frankie Paul*
> *and many more!*
> *It's a 4 compact disc set for only £9.99*
> *At a dealer near you – now!*

Who and Where?
You are young, street wise, a devotee of clubs and club fashion, and skilled at assuming a lower social standing than the one you were born in to. You are at a party or club at which loud music is being played.

What am I saying?
It's a cheap collection of crucial tracks, innit!

When am I saying it?
Probably at night.

When is it going to be broadcast/transmitted?
Evenings and the early hours of the morning.

Why am I saying it?

You are telling people something you think they should know about.

How am I saying it?

You appear to be shouting over the background noise. However, shouting does not work as it can overload the mic and it makes scripts very difficult to understand. The trick is to introduce a lot of tension in to the body by standing stiffly, clenching the fists, and sticking the chin out. If you then deliver the script in a hoarse, throaty voice it sounds like shouting. This script does not call for many upward inflections – the target audience consider them 'cheesy' and are immediately suspicious of any product sold in this way. In some ways, by going against the naturally occurring inflections the excitement is understated. This style was invented by sports commentators who, having whipped themselves into a frenzy, found they had nowhere else to go. As a result they started to underplay moments of excitement, saying such things as: 'He's only scored, hasn't he', with a downward set of inflections.

It's the Greatest Rap & Hardcore Collection ever!!

All the words need to be separated, with pauses after *Greatest* and *Collection*. *Ever* is barked quite aggressively with a downward inflection and an accompanying jabbing pointed finger.

65 Rap & Hardcore originals featuring:

65 can be said through half closed eyes, using the finger for emphasis. *Rap & Hardcore* need to be very clear so that we know what we are dealing with; the 'H' of *Hardcore* can be dropped. *Originals* does need to be lifted in pitch, isolated, and given the benefit of the pointing finger. It needs to be made clear that these are the original tracks by the original artists and not cover versions by unknowns.

Dina Carroll
Simon Harris
Heavy D
Frankie Paul

These four names need to be picked out with increasing, but underplayed, surprise that they can all be found on the same compilation. They can be imagined to be names on an enormous poster so that you point to each one before reading it out.

and many more!

This includes an added value word – *and* needs to be isolated and emphasised. *Many more* should be overplayed and not thrown away.

It's a 4 compact disc set for only £9.99

This is not easy to say. *4* needs to be slightly lifted and isolated; the 'c' on the end of *disc* can hardly be pronounced without detracting from the street credentials; and there should be a pause after *only*. The price is emphasised and is said as 'nine pound ninety nine'.

At a dealer near you – now!

The 't' is lost at the end of *at*; the finger should point at the listener on *you*; and there must be a pause before delivering an elongated *now*. Ideally, the last word should disappear into repeat echo.

HARGREAVES OF TAUNTON – Comic Horror

This is a 40-second radio commercial for a male or female voice. The original sound effects track is on the CD. The midnight sale is a popular device in both the UK and the USA. The advertising for these events is nearly always humorous and features ghosts, vampires, witches or monsters. This script is no exception! This kind of commercial is usually found on local radio stations.

> *Something very odd is happening tonight at 100 High Street, Taunton.*
> *'Tis the night for Moonlight Madness at Hargreaves of Taunton.*
> *Their doors open at 6pm sharp for six hours of unrepeatable price reductions on some of the finest floor coverings in Zummerzett – with interest-free credit – right through till midnight! Written credit details on request.*
> *Tonight – starting 6pm at Hargreaves of Taunton.*
> *It would be madness to miss it!*

Who and Where?
For a male voice, the characterisation should be in the style of Long John Silver from *Treasure Island*. A female voice could be a comic witch, complete with cackle. The FX track starts with midnight in the graveyard and ends with a clap of thunder. In between there are owls, howling winds, and weird noises. You can be in a graveyard, in a cave, cavorting skyclad beside a bonfire, or in the woods. The voice-over should be in moderate reverb to add to the effects.

What am I saying?
You are telling us about a fun event, taking place after normal shop hours, and offering a chance to pick up a bargain.

When am I saying it?
In the early hours of the morning on the day of the sale.

When is it going to be broadcast/transmitted?
Morning, noon and night for a couple of days before the sale – there will be different versions of the script saying 'tomorrow' or 'this Friday', as appropriate. 'Tonight' is the final script to be broadcast.

Why am I saying it?
To attract customers!

How am I saying it?
If male, the Long John Silver approach is quite funny and not threatening. The idea is to attract customers, not frighten them away – the humour must shine through. The female witch is a universally popular character – she is more 'intimate' and close miked than her male counterpart.

Something very odd is happening tonight

The script should have quite an energetic start, immediately after the second tolling bell. The witch can be very precise about *Something very odd*, delivering it with a suspicious curiosity. The male can change *Something* to the more colloquial *Summat* or even *Zummat*! There needs to be a pause both before and after *tonight* – the listeners need to know when the sale takes place.

at 100 High Street, Taunton.

Many people say '100' as 'a hundred'. In the land of voice-over it is 'one hundred' – in the same way that 200 is 'two hundred'. For obvious reasons the address and the name of the town need to be clear. *Taunton* needs to be lifted.

'Tis the night for Moonlight Madness at Hargreaves of Taunton.

'Tis is best suited to Long John – the Witch might care to change *'Tis* to 'It's'. *Moonlight Madness* should be enjoyed, perhaps letting a little hint of madness show through. The shop name – *Hargreaves* should be emphasised rather than *Taunton* because we already know where we are from the first line. Long John might choose to drop the initial 'H' from *Hargreaves*.

Their doors open at 6pm sharp

Both characters like the word *sharp*, so isolate it and enjoy it!

for six hours of unrepeatable price reductions

This needs to come across very clearly, with an upward inflection.

on some of the finest floor coverings in Zummerzett

A slight feeling of making an announcement brings this to life.

with interest free credit – right through till midnight!

Delivered in a slightly 'crafty' and confidential tone of voice – you are giving the listener an insider's tip! Enjoy the word *midnight*; it is one of your favourite times.

Written credit details on request.

This is a legal necessity and does not sell – it is usually thrown away as quickly as possible. However, either of these two characters can turn it to their advantage. Make it defiant, daring the listener to ask!

Tonight – starting 6pm at Hargreaves of Taunton.

Isolate and emphasise *Tonight* by sticking a bony finger in the air. Lift *starting 6pm* and give *Hargreaves* and *Taunton* equal pitch and emphasis.

It would be madness to miss it!

This is a comic threat with the implication that something unfortunate might happen to you if you miss it. End with a comic laugh or cackle which, if you get the timing right, will be interrupted by the clap of thunder.

INVICTA MOTORS – A Zany Musical Ditty

This script is for someone not scared to work with music. It is half sung and half spoken, but the voice has to be perfectly synchronised with the music; there is no margin for error. This was originally a TV commercial in which the emphasis was on comedy. Everything went wrong: cars would not start, salesmen dressed as villains, wheels came off, comedy gangsters appeared, and terrible old bangers were offered in part exchange. It can be a male or female voice.

Invicta motors will sell to you
Second-hand cars that drive like new
We wash'em polish'em service'em too
Drive to Invicta Motors

Big ones small ones sports cars too
Red ones white ones green and blue
Take your pick there's a car for you
Drive to Invicta Motors

Guarantee warrantee part-exchange
Finance Bank Loans we'll arrange
For second-hand cars we've got the range
Drive to Invicta Motors

Who and Where?

You are an unseen comic performer providing the song, which works on its own but which, for the purpose of television, is accompanied by a very zany film.

What am I saying?

You are entertaining the audience by presenting an old, established, and highly respected chain of garages as a bunch of complete nitwits.

When am I saying it?

No specific time.

When is it going to be broadcast/transmitted?

Peak family viewing times.

Why am I saying it?

To attract new customers, entertain existing ones, and provide a talking point which will increase the public profile of the garage.

How am I saying it?

As zanily as is believably possible, consistent with clarity.

A piece such as this would be demoed first and the demo sent to the voice artist for him or her to learn. It is too complicated to write performance notes to cover it. There is a demo performance on the CD as well as the backing track. Learn it by 'singing' along with the voice on the demo performance and then attempt it as a solo performance using the voiceless backing track. It was originally recorded as three separate sections rather than one complete performance.

BLACK MAGIC CHOCOLATES – Soft, Sexy Sell

This is a script that everyone wants to get hold of and have a go at. It is an extremely well-written script that is difficult to get right without making yourself sound ridiculous. It is a radio and television script for a male or female voice. It lasts 40 seconds and a music backing track can be found on the CD.

Do you know the secret of the Black Magic Box?
No?

Then I'll tell you.

Every chocolate is covered with a mouth-watering plain chocolate coating, and filled with a delicious fruit cream that melts into perfection the moment it passes your lips.

That's why a box of Black Magic – given to the one you love – shows how much you care.

Black Magic – your secret's safe with us.

Who and Where?

You are a seducer – male or female – on the prowl. You are wherever such people ply their trade – in an hotel, in a cocktail bar, at a party, or in a casino.

What am I saying?

You are saying that Black Magic chocolates are one of life's indulgences, best enjoyed in secret, between consenting adults. Once having partaken it is not necessary to discuss the indulgence.

When am I saying it?

Probably in the evening.

When is it going to be broadcast/transmitted?

Definitely in the evening!

Why am I saying it?

For your own nefarious purposes and to introduce others to your particular indulgence.

How am I saying it?

Very smoothly and sexily. The script is delivered very close to the mic; you wouldn't want anyone to overhear, would you?

Do you know the secret of the Black Magic Box?

This is a question and should be addressed to one specific person. It must sound like a question. The *you* must be very gently focused and lifted in pitch. The general pitch then descends to *Black Magic Box*, whereupon it rises again with each successive word.

No?

One word which, in this context, conveys so much meaning. The person asked has said 'no' to the initial question. You, the questioner, then repeat the answer, unable to disguise your surprise and excitement at the admission. You have found someone at last! This word needs an even bigger turn than *gin* did in the first example in this chapter.

73

Then I'll tell you.

Of course you will – you've been searching for this person and this moment for years! *I'll* must be isolated and *tell you* given a rising inflection.

Every chocolate is covered with a mouth-watering plain chocolate coating,

This long and difficult sentence sees you entering a momentary rapture as you wax lyrical about the quality of Black Magic chocolates. It is worth considering the possible significance of *covering, filling* and *melting in to perfection the moment it passes your lips.* This first part of the sentence starts with a trap for the unwary. If you stress *chocolate* rather than *every* you imply that there might be something else in the box which is not covered in chocolate. Stress *every* and the chocolates become the sole contents of the box. The pitch must rise gently towards *coating.* You might need to take a breath here, although it is possible to do the whole sentence in one breath. If you can't it is worth practising until you can!

and filled with a delicious fruit cream that melts into perfection

Do not make much of the *and*, then drop the pitch on *filled* and gradually bring it up again to *perfection.* Resist the temptation to snatch a breath; pause as you savour the melting into perfection.

the moment it passes your lips.

Best said with the eyes closed. *Lips* should be on an upward inflection.

That's why a box of Black Magic

Pause after *why*, then see and point to *a box of Black Magic*

– given to the one you love –

The overall pitch is slightly lower than the previous line. See and indicate *the one you love.*

shows how much you care.

Elongate *shows*, emphasise *much*, and lift the pitch of *care.*

Black Magic

Said in such a way that it no longer means chocolates but something magical.

Do you know the secret of the Black Magic Box?

No?

Then I'll tell you.

Every chocolate is covered with a mouthwatering plain chocolate coating, and filled with a delicious fruit cream that melts into perfection the moment it passes your lips.

That's why a box of Black Magic - given to the one you love - shows how much you care.

Black Magic - your secret's safe with us.

A script which has been marked up very well. The horizontal arrow over 'Every chocolate' reminds the performer to keep the flow going at this point. Notice, in the last line, how 'safe' has been marked with inverted commas and 'us' has been marked with the musical symbol for a turn – pitching above and below the final pitch of the word.

– your secret's safe with us.

This is said suggestively so that *safe* is the last thing that the *secret* is! Lift *secret's*, follow it with a slight pause, smile and raise the eyebrows when saying *safe*, and give *us* a very suggestive turn.

5

Narration and Corporate Scripts

This chapter features six scripts ranging from a gentle wildlife film to a hard hitting script about safety equipment for fuel tankers. These were all written to go with pictures, but it is part of the skill of a voice-over to make them work as audio only. Remember, the job of the voice-over is to create pictures in the mind of the listener and let them look at them. Television programmes use sound to seduce the listener in to 'watching' – many television sets are left on all day and are only watched when something 'sounds interesting'.

When you have studied and practised the analysis of each script you should try reading them against the relevant backing track. It is a very good exercise to try to do them in one take – without stopping or making mistakes. This does not reflect current methods of working as technology allows us to edit together a final performance from a large number of imperfect versions. However, if you can perform a script in a small number of takes you are much more likely to be booked for another job. There are many stories of famous actors being less than competent in the voice-over studio. Their lack of skill is tolerated only because they are a 'name'. Unknowns are not treated so kindly!

Narration scripts rely for their success on the performer reacting to the world they are talking about. Everything being referred to must be given a 'place' in which it exists. These places are then looked at or pointed to when the 'thing' is referred to. This creates the illusion that the voice-over is really 'there' and not standing in front of a microphone in a dingy basement studio. In the analysis of these scripts you will be instructed to 'see', 'look', and 'point' – these actions are performed in front of the microphone without actually seeing the pictures which accompany the script.

BIRDS OF THE SEASHORE – A Natural History Script

Narrating a natural history film is often one of the main ambitions of people entering the voice business. It is not a task that it is often entrusted to beginners.

Wildlife films are, at best, a contrivance. Many are shot mute (filmed without sound). It may be possible to get a miniature camera into a difficult location but it is not always possible to get sound recording equipment into the same small space. The soundtrack may be recorded at the same time but independently of the film, or on a completely different occasion. It may even be totally fabricated from sound effects discs and noises created in the recording studio. If you listen carefully to a wildlife film with your eyes closed, you may well be able to hear the sound recordist's arms sloshing about in baby baths full of water, or their bare feet treading on piles of old recording tape! Recording tape makes the most authentic undergrowth rustle known to modern microphones. The narrator is expected to be part of this contrivance – pretending to be part of the action – but just out of camera shot. We cannot see them but we know that if only we could look a little bit to the left, they would be found lying under a bush, microphone in hand, determined not to scare the animals away.

Wildlife scripts are mostly recorded in the studio, very often without the voice artist being asked to watch the film. Modern studio equipment such as Timeline can, within reason, stretch or shrink different areas of the recorded script to match the timing of the edited film. All the voice artist has to do is deliver the script in hushed tones and convince us that they are really there by 'seeing' the things they are talking about.

This is part of a script dealing with birds of the seashore. The music and effects are on the CD; the script is designed to last the entire length of the M&E track – 2 minutes 5 seconds. The voice starts after the first phrase of music. The script, like the music, has a beginning, a middle, and an end. It can, of course feature a male or female voice.

> *Birds are perhaps the most easily observed inhabitants of the seashore. Gulls, for instance, betray their presence with their screeching cries long before they can be seen paddling near the water's edge or sitting out on the breakwaters. There is but one reason for this abundance of birds – food. The seashore provides them with an extremely rich source of nourishment.*
>
> *Many species of wading birds gather, in large numbers, to feed. A few, such as the knot and dunlin, congregate in vast*

flocks thousands strong, twisting and turning together over the waves in a breathtaking aerial ballet.

Terns, looking like large white swallows, hover over the surface then plunge downwards, emerging with an eel or sprat. The large black and white gannet feeds in similar fashion but dives from an enormous height, causing a considerable splash. Shags and cormorants dive from the water's surface but can also be seen sitting on the rocks, their wings stretched out to dry in the sun. The gulls, the opportunists of the birdworld, can be found on quaysides, squabbling over scraps.

A visit to the seashore, perhaps during a holiday trip, inevitably involves dipping into rock pools, turning over stones and peering at the colourful creatures that live underneath them. But look up, and watch the birds, for they are equally fascinating in their diversity and behaviour.

Who and Where?
You are yourself, standing on the seafront in a West Country fishing village.

What am I saying?
You are enthusing about sea birds and encouraging us to be more observant.

When am I saying it?
Daytime

When is it going to be broadcast/transmitted?
During the afternoon on satellite television.

Why am I saying it?
For the purposes of education and entertainment.

How am I saying it?
Quietly – close to the mic.

Birds

The hardest word in the script! The listener has no idea what you are going to be talking about and this one word tells them most of what they want to know. The delivery has to be 'up', because birds are thought of as being in the sky and because it conveys your enthusiasm for the subject. If you give the word a turn, use a hand gesture to point to a bird, then pause, you should create the desired effect. It is quite acceptable for someone to have 20 or 30 attempts at getting this one word to their satisfaction.

are perhaps the most easily observed inhabitants of the seashore.

Good diction is important for this line, and throughout the script. Lift *inhabitants*, and pause afterwards. *Of the seashore* is very important because it tells the listener where we are and what kind of birds we might expect to see and talk about. As you say *seashore*, point to it. It is about 100 metres away from you so the inflection is up. If we were on a clifftop the inflection would be down.

Gulls, for instance,

From the generality of 'birds' and 'the seashore' we now focus our attention on one particular species and one specific bird. Point to them as you say *gulls*. Pause and drop the pitch before shrugging your shoulders and saying *for instance*.

betray their presence with their screeching cries

The pitch comes back up and the slight emphasis is on *betray* and not *presence*. Get this the wrong way round and it will sound as though the birds are laden with gifts! Be slightly lyrical about *screeching cries* – the two words can have a very gentle downward pitch change. Pause slightly before the next line.

long before they can be seen

Pick up the pitch and the energy and lift *seen*.

paddling near the water's edge or sitting out on the breakwaters.

Here the two locations have to be very clearly shown to be in different places. Pause after *water's edge* to give you time to change your field of vision before saying *sitting out on the breakwaters*. Breakwaters are further away than the water's edge so they have a higher pitch. Objects that are further away are higher in our field of vision; objects at our feet have a low pitch.

There is but one reason for this abundance of birds – food.

Sound a little philosophical here. *Birds* is slightly up and followed by a pause. *Food* can be either up or down: up to be philosophical and down to be practical.

The seashore provides them with an extremely rich source of nourishment.

This is philosophical or practical depending on the mood struck in the previous line. This line marks the end of the first train of thought.

Many species of wading birds gather, in large numbers, to feed.

This is where the fun starts! There now follows a catalogue of seven different birds or groups of birds. It is a catalogue through which the voice must browse, maintaining the feeling of the list but greeting each new bird with fresh interest and telling us a fascinating fact about it. The script becomes an exercise in visualisation and 'placing' things. *Wading birds* needs to be lifted to show us this interesting group – there they are, out in the estuary! Pause after *gather* and again after *numbers*. Lift *feed*.

A few, such as the knot and dunlin, congregate in vast flocks thousands strong,

Lift *few* and put *knot and dunlin* in different places, preferably to your left and right. Lift *vast flocks* then pause before being slightly overawed at *thousands strong*.

twisting and turning together over the waves in a breathtaking aerial ballet.

This whole line needs to be up on a little plateau as you stand there gazing into the sky, wondering at the antics of these marvellous birds.

Terns, looking like large white swallows,

At this point we meet a new species of bird so there has to be the split second pause while we decide which one it is. The delivery for *terns* is very similar to *birds* at the beginning. *Looking like large white swallows* is not part of the main body of information and could be removed from the script without affecting the overall sense. It is known, rightly or wrongly, as a subclause. It is important to convey this slightly lower status as the listener is always subconsciously on the look-out for pieces of information that they do not have to try and remember. The standard way of conveying this is by raising the shoulders when saying it. Raising the shoulders gives a short sentence or phrase a completely different feel from the main body of the script. If you give this particular subclause the wrong inflection you end up with two groups of terns – the ordinary ones and those that make a point of disguising themselves as large white swallows!

hover over the surface then plunge downwards, emerging with an eel or sprat.

This is an act which starts with stillness and continues with a sudden burst of movement. This has to be conveyed in the voice. *Plunge* requires energy but not volume. We are talking about *terns* in the plural so when they emerge with an *eel or sprat* there should be two of them to look at – one to the left and one to the right.

The large black and white gannet feeds in similar fashion

Here is another bird in the list. Think of the name as being *black and white gannet* rather than just *gannet*, it is more interesting to listen to. Pause after *gannet* and lift *feeds* and *fashion*.

but dives from an enormous height, causing a considerable splash.

This bird is much higher up in the air than the tern so really lift *enormous height*. You have to bring us down to sea level during the dive, however. Start your descent during the word *causing* and end it on *splash*.

Shags and cormorants dive from the water's surface

Two new birds in two slightly different places – lift *surface* to distinguish their diving habits from those of the previous two species.

but can also be seen sitting on the rocks, their wings stretched out to dry in the sun.

The mood slightly softens here as the activities become more peaceful. Pause after *rocks* and be slightly more lyrical on *stretched out to dry in the sun*.

The gulls, the opportunists of the birdworld, can be found on quaysides, squabbling over scraps.

This is the last of the list. The subclause – *the opportunists of the birdworld* – can be made interesting by smiling through it as you enjoy the antics of these loveable rogues. See and place the *quaysides* before smiling again for *squabbling over scraps*.

A visit to the seashore, perhaps during a holiday trip

This is the third train of thought and requires a slightly renewed attack. Stress *visit* rather than *seashore* because we already know where we are. *Perhaps during a holiday trip* is a subclause and time for some shoulder exercise as previously described – stress *holiday* and not *trip*. Stressing the latter would make it sound like an unfortunate stumble rather than a pleasurable diversion!

inevitably involves dipping into rock pools,

In order not to make this sound too 'read', hesitate after *inevitably involves* while you decide exactly what it does inevitably involve. Keep *dipping into rock pools* up and really see them.

turning over stones and peering at the colourful creatures that live underneath them.

Hesitate and pause as you turn over the stones and see what's living there and keep the flow going beyond *them* – ignore the full stop.

But look up, and watch the birds,

Now you have to take both yourself and the listener from poking about in a rock pool to gazing up to the sky, so *look up*! Deliver *birds* with a sense of awe.

for they are equally fascinating in their diversity and behaviour.

This has to convey the feeling of being the end of the script without losing interest or energy. Nodding throughout it and pausing after *fascinating* and *diversity* will help. *And* is an added value word so put a gentle turn in it and pause before saying *behaviour* with an upward inflection. Ideally, the last word of the script should coincide with the last note of the music. It may take some practice to be able to do this – the trick is to adjust the length of the last paragraph when you have got to know the music. It is hard to do but when it happens it is pure spine tingling magic!

TANKER SAFETY – Hard Hitting Safety Film

This is the commentary from a film produced to promote the safety equipment that can be fitted to road tankers to prevent the spillage of dangerous or flammable liquids. The music track is on the CD. A male or female voice can be used, although it is likely to be a man who is asked to perform a script like this.

In Britain today there are millions of miles of roads used by countless numbers of motor cars each travelling an average of 12,000 miles a year. There are heavy lorries for transporting goods, tens of thousands of buses, and many other vehicles. Aircraft alone use massive amounts of aviation fuel and every week thousands of ships leave European ports. All have internal combustion engines consuming hydrocarbon fuels.

69 per cent of households have central heating, many of which use oil, and industry depends on oil to power and lubricate machinery. Most of these essential fuels are delivered by road in tankers – each carrying up to 44 thousand litres of highly flammable product.

Any one of these vehicles could present a major hazard. Fortunately, legislation demands stringent safety standards and road and rail tankers are designed and built to these high standards.

The drivers of these vehicles are highly trained, skilled and responsible people.

Nevertheless, accidents happen.

Who and Where?

You are a spokesperson for the company, but not part of it.

What am I saying?
You are raising the listener's awareness of a problem they may not even have thought of. You will, of course, offer a solution.

When am I saying it?
No specific time.

When is it going to be broadcast/transmitted?
At seminars, meetings, conferences, and trade shows. It is unlikely to be shown on television.

Why am I saying it?
As discussed, somebody once defined advertising as 'taking away people's self-respect and sense of security and selling it back to them, at a price!' This kind of script might be considered to be guilty of this.

How am I saying it?
Quite forcefully.

In Britain today

This is a very popular opening with scriptwriters and their clients. It has a feeling of importance. It also sets the scene very quickly.

there are millions of miles of roads

Keep the pitch up and try to see at least some of them.

used by countless numbers of motor cars

Imagine a crowded motorway – do not go down.

each travelling an average of 12,000 miles a year.

Again, keep the flow and the energy going.

There are heavy lorries for transporting goods,

See them – in a specific place.

tens of thousands of buses,

See and place these in a different place.

and many other vehicles.

This does not include an added value word. Make the *many other vehicles* as important as the buses and lorries.

Aircraft alone use massive amounts of aviation fuel

Separate *Aircraft* from *alone* to prevent it from sounding like a dating agency for Jumbo Jets. Keep *fuel* up.

and every week thousands of ships leave European ports.

See, lift and place the ships. Do not go down on *ports.*

All have internal combustion engines consuming hydrocarbon fuels.

Stress *all* and *internal combustion engines.* Pause before *consuming* and lift *hydrocarbon fuels.*

69 per cent of households have central heating,

This is a new thought. Lift *households* and *central heating.*

many of which use oil,

Slightly emphasise *many* and *oil.*

and industry depends on oil

Pause after *industry* and emphasise *depends on oil.*

to power and lubricate machinery.

Isolate *power* and *lubricate,* and see and lift *machinery.*

Most of these essential fuels

Emphasise *most* and *essential fuels.*

are delivered by road in tankers –

Pause after *delivered* and again after *road* and *tankers.*

each carrying up to 44 thousand litres of highly flammable product.

This should be a slightly dramatic statement and very 'up'.

Any one of these vehicles could present a major hazard.

Emphasise *one, could,* and *major hazard.* This is the area designed to worry the listener.

Fortunately, legislation demands stringent safety standards

Emphasise *fortunately* and be very precise about *stringent safety standards.*

and road and rail tankers are designed and built to these high standards.

Slow up on this line and pause slightly after *built.* Emphasise *high standards.*

The drivers of these vehicles are highly trained, skilled and responsible people.

Keep all of this lifted – almost in the style of a citation.

Nevertheless, accidents happen.

All three words should be equally spaced, equally pitched, and mildly dramatic. Do not elongate any of the words.

VITILIGO – A Medical Documentary

Highly technical medical films are the province of specialists – usually qualified medical practitioners who also do voice-overs. An incorrect inflection from an uninformed voice-over artist can alter the meaning for an informed and trained audience. This script is from a film designed to educate and inform parents, so it was not given to a medical specialist to read. The voice can be male or female – the original was female. There is a suitable M&E track on the CD.

> *Vitiligo should not be presented as a 'disease' which it is not – but for what it really is – a condition. It is a condition in which the skin loses its pigment. The range of human conditions is as many and varied as the population of the world and no two of us are exactly the same. We can be any combination of short, tall, fat, thin, dark-skinned, fair-skinned, short sighted, diabetic, lame, super-intelligent, physically strong . . . the list is endless. Vitiligo should be presented in the context of this range of conditions.*
>
> *Children – like adults – can be cruel and will very often 'pick on' certain of the characteristics of their peers. This behaviour seems to have been natural to children throughout the ages and it would be ridiculous to suggest that a video film will change this.*

Who and Where?
You are a sympathetic medical advisor giving people information which will, you hope, prevent a particular problem. You are not in a specific place – you are simply providing the voice-over.

What am I saying?
Vitiligo is a condition in which patches of skin lose their pigment. This results in white patches – particularly noticeable and distressing for dark-skinned people. People who have the condition lose their natural protection against sunburn and have to cover up or stay in the shade. Sufferers feel very self-conscious and find the stares and remarks that they attract hard to deal with. In some cultures people with the condition are shunned as it is wrongly thought to be a communicable disease. This script explains that Vitiligo is a condition and not a disease and, like all conditions, is part of the

human experience. It acknowledges the fact that children can be cruel and will probably be so to a child with this condition. The film sets out to educate the audience into an understanding of the condition in the hope that they might pass this on to their own children.

When am I saying it?
No specific time.

When is it going to be broadcast/transmitted?
It is shown in schools when a child is admitted with this condition. It is also shown to the parents.

Why am I saying it?
To educate people and prevent problems.

How am I saying it?
With understanding for the problems and fears of both sides.

Vitiligo

Again, the 'problem' of the first word in the script. If you record this piece for a voice tape the listener will have no idea what they are going to be confronted with. Most people have never heard or seen this word. It has to be delivered in a way which says, 'Yes, I know this is a difficult word, I'm going to make it as easy as possible for you, and I would be grateful if you would just stick with me for a few minutes because you will learn something interesting'. The pronunciation is Vitty-lie-go, with the stress on the 'lie' in the middle. Say it as if you are indicating the word on a poster.

should not be presented as a 'disease'

A positive negative – smile as you say it. Indicate the inverted commas around *'disease'* by miming them in the air as you say the word. This will create the necessary brief pause before you say it and will help lift the word.

which it is not

The continuation of the positive negative – lift *not*.

but for what it really is – a condition

The emphasis is on *really*. Lift *condition*.

It is a condition in which the skin loses its pigment.

Pause after *condition*, place *skin* and pause afterwards, then lift *pigment*.

The range of human conditions is as many and varied as the population of the world

Put a slight emphasis on *range*, lift and pause after *conditions*, slow up for and separate *many and varied*. Give *world* an upward inflection.

and no two of us are exactly the same.

Yet another positive negative. Pause slightly after *two of us.*

We can be any combination of

Lift *any* and give this line a slightly philosophical feel – outstretched arms with upturned palms will help. Leave *of* slightly hanging as you look around to 'see' the first example in the list.

short, tall, fat, thin, dark-skinned, fair-skinned, short sighted, diabetic, lame, super-intelligent, physically strong – the list is endless.

This is a long list of conditions and is in danger of being boring if badly handled. Lists are a particular problem in narration scripts. Scriptwriters, or their clients, nearly always insist on the lists being long. In this case the way of dealing with the eleven different conditions is to 'see' an example of each. Imagine a long line of children passing in front of you – as they pass, pick out a few for comment. Do it lovingly and avoid 'commenting' on them. Don't make *fat* or *tall* sound any more or less desirable than *thin* or *short*. As you go through the list get a little faster until you can deliver *the list is endless* with a well-deserved smile.

Vitiligo should be presented in the context of this range of conditions.

Vitiligo must be said carefully, with the rest of the line delivered quite caringly. The emphases are on *should, context,* and *range.*

Children – like adults – can be cruel

Said with sensitivity. Put *children* and *adults* in different places. Do not let *cruel* drop in pitch but try to give it a slightly plaintive sound.

and will very often 'pick on' certain of the characteristics of their peers.

Isolate *'pick on'* and again indicate the inverted commas with your fingers. If you do not, the words become lost and hard to understand. Pause after *characteristics* and keep the inflection of *peers* up.

This behaviour seems to have been natural to children throughout the ages

The stress is better on *This* than on *behaviour* – it maintains the flow. *Natural* and *ages* need slight lifts in pitch.

and it would be ridiculous to suggest that a video film will change this.

Lift *ridiculous* and *suggest*. Pause after *suggest*, and again after *video film*, which should be treated as one word. Smile for *will change this* but do not go down – leave it hanging.

THIN WALLED TUBE – A Technical Script

This script describes the workings of an extrusion machine – or does it? It is a wonderful exercise in visualisation – seeing (or even imagining!) what is happening and communicating it to the listener.

It works like this:

The machine consists of a wheel with a circumferential groove, and a pivotal shoe. This shoe houses the extrusion tool which comprises an entry block, die abutment, and an extrusion die. The shoe is raised so the tooling covers part of the wheel circumference to form a continuous extrusion chamber between the wheel groove and the tooling. When the feed rod is entered into the wheel it is driven around the groove by friction until it meets the abutment. The combination of heat and pressure generated by friction in the groove allows the material to be extruded through the die, thus forming a continuously extruded product.

This mode of operation has been further developed to enable the machine to accept two feed stock rods which allows increased production rates and the ability to extrude thin walled tube in various aluminium alloys.

Who and Where?
You are the inventor of the machine, you are standing beside it pointing out the various features and explaining how it works.

What am I saying?
The machine makes thin walled tube in various aluminium alloys – continuous pipes without seams or joins.

When am I saying it?
No specific time.

When is it going to be broadcast/transmitted?
When explaining how the machine works to potential customers or visiting engineers.

Why am I saying it?
Perhaps to increase sales.

How am I saying it?
Slowly, but with commitment and enthusiasm.

It works like this:

Pause after *works* and point to the machine as you say *this* so that you end on a slightly higher pitch.

The machine consists of a wheel

Point to the machine and then point up to the wheel.

with a circumferential groove,

Which means that it is like a large bicycle wheel without the tyre on. Keep *groove* up.

and a pivotal shoe.

Put a slight turn in *and*, drop the pitch for pivotal, and bring it up again for *shoe.*

This shoe houses the extrusion tool

Lift *shoe* again and then lift *extrusion tool.*

which comprises an entry block, die abutment, and an extrusion die.

This is a list of the component parts of the extrusion tool and each one needs to be pointed out and assigned a 'place'. Pause slightly on *and.* Do not go down on *die.*

The shoe is raised

Point out the shoe and make sure that *raised* is raised!

so the tooling covers part of the wheel circumference

Lift *tooling* and *wheel circumference.*

to form a continuous extrusion chamber

Keep *continuous extrusion chamber* up with a slight stress on the *tru* of *extrusion*

between the wheel groove and the tooling.

Point out the *wheel groove* emphasis and slightly pause on the *and.* Keep the inflection of *tooling* up.

When the feed rod is entered into the wheel

89

This is the first time we have heard about the *feed rod* so it must be pointed out as something new. Place the *feed rod* over to one side, then move to the other side as it approaches the wheel. Simply move the head slowly from left to right during this line.

it is driven around the groove by friction

Put a slight emphasis on *around* and pause after *groove*. Do not go down on *friction*.

until it meets the abutment.

Be precise about *meets* – use a pointing finger. Raise the eyebrows while saying *the abutment*.

The combination of heat and pressure

This is a new thought. *Heat and pressure* must be separated, given equal weight, and not rolled into one.

generated by friction in the groove

The emphasis is on *friction* and *groove* is lifted.

allows the material to be extruded through the die,

Pause slightly after *extruded* and emphasise *through*.

thus forming a continuously extruded product.

Pause after *thus forming* and give the words *continuously extruded product* equal weight and pitch.

This mode of operation

This is another new thought and the emphasis is on *operation*.

has been further developed

Emphasis on *further*; *developed* must not go down.

to enable the machine to accept two feed stock rods

Pause after *machine* and lift the pitch of *two* and *rods*.

which allows increased production rates

Pause after *allows* and lift *increased production rates* as a definite benefit.

and the ability to extrude thin walled tube

Do not emphasise *and*, and pause after *ability* and also after *extrude*. Be very precise about the diction for *thin walled tube* and give each of the three words equal pitch and weight.

in various aluminium alloys.

Slow up here to signal the end by putting equal pauses after *various* and *aluminium*. *Alloys* can go slightly down in pitch.

QUINTA DA ROSA – A Travelogue

This is the script for a leisure company's promotional film and is designed to persuade holidaymakers to book themselves into the Quinta da Rosa development. The original film used a female voice but a male voice would be equally acceptable. This is a very interesting script and would serve well as a test piece for sight-reading. It has been known to take up to one hour to record the second paragraph satisfactorily. There is a music and effects track for this script on the CD.

> *Lisbon – situated on the banks of the River Tagus – is regarded as one of Europe's most beautiful cities. With its tree-lined avenues, elegant squares, and numerous places of interest, Lisbon is a popular attraction, providing the sophistication of a capital city for holidaymakers at Quinta da Rosa. The Portuguese capital is truly a city of contrasts where you will find a combination of new and old with fashionable shopping areas, fine restaurants, and night-spots.*
>
> *Only 35 minutes from Lisbon, with its cosmopolitan culture, and only 20 minutes from the tranquillity of the ancient town of Sintra – 'That glorious Eden' as Byron called it, with its fairytale palaces and gracious gardens and scenic views, lies the coast of Estoril and Cascais. With sky and sea of blue, the waters of the fine sandy beaches vary from light laps, so pleasant for the gentle swimmer, to Hell's Mouth – an outcrop of red rock eaten away by relentless waves.*

Who and Where?
You are a spokesperson for the holiday company concerned. You are at the resort.

What am I saying?
You are saying that Quinta da Rosa is situated in Lisbon which has all the usual attractions of a European capital city. You might also be thought to be saying that there are other, and perhaps more interesting places 35 minutes away. What you do not say is which method of travel is necessary to reach these places in only 35 minutes. You intentionally do not mention distances.

When am I saying it?
In the summertime.

When is it going to be broadcast/transmitted?

It is unlikely to be seen on television. It will be shown at promotional events within the travel industry, within travel agents shops, and probably at time-share meetings.

Why am I saying it?

You are persuading people to book a holiday.

How am I saying it?

Very persuasively.

Lisbon –

The first and hardest word. The natural inclination is to give this word a downward inflection, split between *Lis* and *bon*. This would be wholly inappropriate in this context. The word has to be the answer to an unspoken question. The first short phrase of the music resembles a magic curtain being lifted, we see a romantic city skyline silhouetted against a beautiful sunset. A blue and tranquil sea can be seen glinting in the background. Your listener pauses, and says, 'Where's that then?' You hear this question and answer with a sweeping gesture, an upward inflection, and a smile towards the picture *Lisbon.*

situated on the banks of the River Tagus –

A subclause – lift the shoulders. *Tagus* is pronounced Tay-gush.

is regarded as one of Europe's most beautiful cities.

Add a small pause after *regarded*, and wax slightly lyrical over *one of Europe's most beautiful cities.*

With its tree-lined avenues, elegant squares, and numerous places of interest,

Here is a list of three areas which must all be placed and looked at. Pause slightly after *its*, and lift *interest* because the flow continues after this point.

Lisbon is a popular attraction

There should be a slightly renewed attack on *Lisbon.* Keep *attraction* up.

providing the sophistication of a capital city,

Slight emphasis on *sophistication* and lift *city.*

for holidaymakers at Quinta da Rosa.

Emphasise *holidaymakers* and pause afterwards. *Quinta da Rosa* is pronounced kinter dah roser. Show it to the listener as you say it.

The Portuguese capital is truly a city of contrasts

The emphases are on *capital* and *contrasts*; pause after both. *Truly* can be slightly lifted.

where you will find a combination of new and old

This has already been dealt with briefly in chapter 3: *new and old* exist side by side and should be placed one to the left and one to the right.

with fashionable shopping areas, fine restaurants, and night-spots.

Again, a list of three features each needing to be placed. Do not use a downward inflection on *night-spots* – see undesirable facial eruptions in chapter 3!

Only 35 minutes from Lisbon,

This is the opening part of a sentence containing 46 words! It is difficult to work out the grammatical relationships within this sentence. The solution is to read it with a succession of upward inflections – by the time you get to the end of it the listener will have forgotten exactly what might (or might not) relate to what! The stress in this first line is on *minutes*. It is interesting to try it other ways but anything else will land you in severe difficulties about 30 words later.

with its cosmopolitan culture,

Shoulders up – it's a subclause.

and only 20 minutes from the tranquillity of the ancient town of Sintra

In this line the stress is on *twenty*. *Sintra* must be lifted. It is pronounced as sin-trah.

'That glorious Eden' as Byron called it,

A subclause which also contains a quotation. You can try adopting a 'voice' for Byron, but do not forget to raise your shoulders to achieve the desired subclause effect.

with its fairytale palaces and gracious gardens and scenic views,

Because of the construction of this sentence we do not know whether these delightful places are to be found in Sintra or Cascais. Does this line refer backwards or forwards? Looking at this 46-word sentence as it is written does not give you any idea of the problems involved in saying it! If you have not done so already, read this sentence out loud! The *fairytale palaces, gracious gardens,* and *scenic views* all have to be placed, indicated and looked at. There is one 'and' too many in the line but, as a professional, you have to deal with that. You could always try leaving it out.

lies the coast of Estoril and Cascais.

Pronounced esstorhyl and kaskaysh. If you lift and pause after *Estoril,* then *Cascais* becomes a place on that coast to which we have travelled.

With sky and sea of blue,

It is hard to make this sound convincing! Try waxing lyrical, lifting *blue* and saying the whole line as one beautifully flowing phrase.

the waters of the fine sandy beaches vary

A slight pause on *waters* and *beaches,* then lift *vary.*

from light laps, so pleasant for the gentle swimmer,

Place the *light laps* on one side, ready to balance them against Hell's Mouth – an unusual comparison. *So pleasant for the gentle swimmer* is a subclause.

to Hells Mouth

Make this sound mildly dramatic.

an outcrop of red rock eaten away by relentless waves.

Pause after *red rock,* then give *eaten away by relentless waves* a romantic flavour, and indicate the merciful ending of the script.

LEEDS CASTLE – A Film about an Historic Building

Leeds Castle, found in the southern English county of Kent, is quite rightly described as 'the loveliest castle in the world'. It is like a fairytale castle, 1,000 years old, made of stone, completely surrounded by water, and reached by one of the finest drawbridges you could ever wish to see. The castle is open to visitors and the grounds are used for outdoor events such as symphony and rock concerts, garden parties, and as a launching site for hot air balloons. This script is part of the material used to promote the castle. It was written to go with pictures but is also used as an audio only presentation. The voice can be either male or female. There is a music track to go with this script on the CD.

94

Leeds Castle – one of the most romantic and most ancient castles in the Kingdom. In the 9th century this was the site of a manor of the Saxon royal family. Listed in the Domesday Book, this castle has been a Norman stronghold, a royal residence to six of England's mediaeval Queens, a playground and palace to Henry VIII, and a private home.

Today, lovingly restored and now administered by the Leeds Castle foundation, it is home to a magnificent collection of mediaeval furnishings, paintings, tapestries, and treasures. This is a place where visitors of the present meet with lives of the past.

The castle was first built in stone by Norman barons nearly 900 years ago to overawe the English. On Edward I's accession it was conveyed to the Crown, and for the next three centuries was a royal palace – fortified, enlarged, enriched, and much loved by successive English Kings and Queens.

A past that's not preserved soon becomes a past that is forgotten. Leeds Castle was saved for the nation when Lady Baillie, the last private owner, established the Leeds Castle Foundation on her death in 1974. The objectives of this independent charitable trust are to preserve the castle for important national and international meetings – particularly for the advancement of medical research and for the furtherance of peace – and to promote artistic and cultural events.

Who and Where?
You are a knowledgeable visitor to the castle and quietly very enthusiastic about it. You are walking around the outside and the inside of the castle.

What am I saying?
You are telling us what a wonderful place it is.

When am I saying it?
In the daytime.

When is it going to be broadcast/transmitted?
It will not be broadcast, but it will be shown to visitors, potential visitors, and may be available as a souvenir video.

Why am I saying it?
To promote the interests of the castle.

How am I saying it?
Quietly and with muted enthusiasm.

Leeds Castle

The opening words; introduce the castle by answering the unspoken question with a smile and an upward inflection.

one of the most romantic and most ancient castles in the Kingdom

Be romantic and keep *kingdom* up at the end of the phrase.

In the 9th century this was the site of a manor of the Saxon royal family.

This line contains traps for the unwary. Two paragraphs later the script says *today* as a counterpart to *in the 9th century*, so *9th century* needs to be set up as something with a later significance. *This was the site* refers to the present castle so *this* needs to be isolated and lifted.

Listed in the Domesday Book,

This is a subclause at the beginning of a sentence. The sense is: 'This castle, listed in the Domesday Book, has been a . . .'. The component parts of the sentence have been reversed so you have to start with raised shoulders.

this castle has been

The beginning of a list. Pause slightly before launching into the list, as though deciding which of the many interesting things you are going to start with.

a Norman stronghold, a royal residence to six of England's mediaeval Queens, a playground and palace to Henry VIII, and a private home.

See these different uses as if you are looking at paintings depicting each one. Give each a 'place' and keep the end of the first three points up. The fourth is preceded by an added value *and*, which invites us to marvel at the thought that this massive building was once a private home. *Home* needs to be up.

Today, lovingly restored and now administered by the Leeds Castle foundation,

This line starts with the counterpart of *in the 9th century* and must be given added significance. The rest of this line is another subclause in an unusual place.

it is home to a magnificent collection of

The start of another list.

mediaeval furnishings, paintings, tapestries, and treasures.

See and place these collections. Give a slight lift to the *and* before *treasures*.

This is a place where visitors of the present meet with lives of the past.

This again refers to the castle. Pause after *present* and again after *meet*. Lift *lives* and *past*.

The castle was first built in stone by Norman barons

The Saxon castle was built of wood and the Normans covered this structure with stone. Lift *stone*. *Norman barons* needs a careful inflection to stop it sounding like a firm of modern-day cowboy builders. Stress *barons* rather than *Norman*.

nearly 900 years ago to overawe the English.

Pause after *ago*. Take care to pronounce *overawe* correctly. It must not sound like 'over roar'.

On Edward I's accession it was conveyed to the Crown,

Use the correct diction by putting a very small pause between *Edward I's* and *accession*. It is pronounced 'Edward The First's'. With *conveyed to the Crown*, invoke a feeling of the movement of legal documents.

and for the next three centuries was a royal palace

Stress *palace* and not *royal* because it changed from a castle to a palace.

fortified, enlarged, enriched, and much loved by successive English Kings and Queens.

Another list. See and point to the alterations and make *much loved* a tangible. Give *Kings and Queens* different places but equal weight.

A past that's not preserved soon becomes a past that is forgotten.

Make this sound slightly philosophical. Pause after *preserved* and the second *past* and then lift *forgotten*.

Leeds Castle was saved for the nation

After the last line there is an implied 'however we are pleased to say that'. Lift *Leeds Castle*, *saved*, and *nation*.

when Lady Baillie, the last private owner,

Lift *Lady Baillie* – pronounced 'Bailey'. *The last private owner* is a subclause.

established the Leeds Castle Foundation on her death in 1974.

Make *The Leeds Castle Foundation* very clear. The rest of the line is a positive negative.

The objectives of this independent charitable trust

Lift *trust*.

are

This word needs to be isolated and given a turn. This verb has to refer to the first objective, its related subclause, and then to the second objective!

to preserve the castle for important national and international meetings

Head towards *national and international meetings*.

particularly for the advancement of medical research and for the furtherance of peace

This is a subclause – *peace* needs to be lifted.

and to promote artistic and cultural events.

The first *and* is an added value word. Start to slow up, give *artistic* and *cultural* equal weight, and go down in pitch on *events*. This last word should coincide with the last note of the music.

6

Other Scripts

Here are seven scripts from areas of work other than commercials and narrations. The relevant music for four of them is on the CD – the other three do not use music or sound effects.

COMPUTER SKILLS – A Script for a CD Rom Training Course

This is one of the fastest growing areas of voice work. CD Roms are everywhere and are being given away with everything from breakfast cereals to daily newspapers. The most popular CD Roms, apart from games, are training programmes.

Most people find computers an infuriating but necessary part of daily life. However, they get very annoyed with them when they fail to perform logically. Performing logically is the only thing computers are capable of – the problem is that computers and people have different concepts of logic. Consequently, there is an enormous market for books and CD Roms showing you 'how to get the best (or even anything) out of your computer'.

Books are passive – they do nothing. CD Roms are not passive. They are interactive and create the illusion that you are having a conversation with them. This is, of course, exactly that – an illusion – as they are simply programmed to react to your reactions to their commands. People who get annoyed with computers are equally likely to get annoyed with a talking CD Rom. The voices engaged to perform these scripts therefore have to be very calm, helpful, and able to convey the subliminal message that 'even you can manage this'! The voices can be either male or female – sometimes both are used on the same programme. These scripts are not recorded to music, although there may be the occasional fanfare to reward a correctly completed exercise!

If you wish to save your document you must first click on the 'file' drop-down menu. The 'file' drop-down menu is situated at the top left-hand corner of your screen. Use the mouse to move the cursor until it is over the word 'file'. Then, click once on the left mouse button. You will now be able to see the options on the 'file' drop-down menu.

There are two 'Save' options on this menu – 'Save' and 'Save As'. If this is a new document and you are saving it for the first time you must press 'Save As'. However, if you press 'Save' the computer will realise that this is a new and previously unsaved document and it will automatically show you the 'Save As' menu. The purpose of this menu is to ask you where you want to save the document, and what you want to call it.

At the top left of the menu you will see the words 'Save As' in white letters on a blue background. Underneath this you will see the words 'Save In' and to the right of them is a window with a downward pointing arrow in its right-hand corner. Move the cursor until it is over the arrow and then click on the left mouse button. You will now be able to see a list of the different places where your document can be saved.

Who and Where?
You are a friendly and helpful but disembodied voice.

What am I saying?
You are telling the listener that using a computer is not really hard and that, if only they follow your instructions, they will be able to master it.

When am I saying it?
No specific time.

When is it going to be broadcast/transmitted?
The course can be studied whenever the user chooses.

Why am I saying it?
To encourage the student to persevere.

How am I saying it?
Very patiently, simply, and encouragingly, without sounding condescending. This script requires very strong visualisation skills – you have to guide people to different areas of the screen with your inflections as much as with your instructions. You can repeat 'top left' six times and the student will still be looking in the wrong

place. Get the body language and the inflection right and they will follow you anywhere. Once they have subconsciously learned the pitch difference between your 'left' and 'right' they will be looking in the correct place long before you've finished the instruction.

If you wish to save your document you must first click on the 'file' drop-down menu.

The words *'save'*, *'click'* and *'file'* must be slightly lifted in pitch to emphasise them. Indicate the inverted commas for *'file'* with your fingers – this helps to distinguish it from the other drop-down menus such as Edit, View, Insert, etc. The sentence has to end with an upward inflection to make it clear that further instructions are to follow.

The 'file' drop-down menu is situated at the top left-hand corner of your screen.

The *'file'* drop-down menu is an exact repeat of what was said in the previous line so it can be delivered a little more quickly this time. Pause after *is situated* to let the listener put their brain into gear. Deliver *top left-hand corner* quite slowly and deliberately and point to it yourself. Relax a little on *of your screen*.

Use the mouse to move the cursor until it is over the word 'file'. Then, click once on the left mouse button.

Lift *mouse* to draw attention to it – the listener may have forgotten what it is! Slow up a little for *cursor*. Lift *'file'*. Pause after *then*, and be very clear about *once*, *left*, and *button*.
    This section asks the participant to do something. They can do it correctly, incorrectly, or ignore the instruction. If they do it incorrectly or do nothing the training programme is designed to say *I think we should try that again* or *That was not correct – let's do that section again*. These phrases will also have been recorded by the voice-over artist and will prefix a repeat of the original instruction. If the participant keeps getting this manoeuvre wrong they will hear the same short passage of text several times. This has the potential to be infuriating to someone who is already feeling bad about themselves because they are making mistakes. Not only does the voice used have to be very sympathetic, but everything has to be inflected in such a way that different sections can be joined together without the 'joins' sounding unnatural.

You will now be able to see the options on the 'file' drop-down menu.

Lift *see* and *on*.

There are two 'Save' options on this menu – 'Save' and 'Save As'.

Indicate the inverted commas for the first *'Save'* only. Make sure that *'Save'* and *'Save As'* are shown clearly to be two different options. The *'As'* of *'Save As'* must not drop in pitch because it is encouraging you to choose a file name.

If this is a new document

Lift *new*.

and you are saving it for the first time

Lift *first time*.

you must press 'Save As'.

Lift *'Save As'*.

However if you press 'Save'

Lift *'Save'* slightly.

the computer will realise that this is a new and previously unsaved document

Lift *new* and *unsaved* and do not go down on *document*.

and it will automatically connect you to the 'Save As' menu.

Lift *automatically* and *'Save As'* and pause before saying *menu*.

The purpose of this menu is to ask you where you want to save the document,

We are now looking at the new menu so it is important to emphasise *this*. Lift and pause after *where*.

and what you want to call it.

The *and* needs emphasising because *where* and *what* in this line are of equal importance. Drop the pitch of *it* slightly.

At the top left of the menu you will see the words 'Save As'

See and point to *top left* and slightly lift *'Save As'*.

in white letters on a blue background.

Slow up slightly to keep the listener with you. Make the colour scheme clear by lifting *white* and *blue background*.

Underneath this you will see the words 'Save In'

Stress *underneath* and not *this*. *'Save In'* is important because we have not seen these words before, but leave them hanging because the sense carries on into the next line.

and to the right of them is a window

Lead the listener to the right, and lift *them* and *window*.

with a downward pointing arrow in its right hand corner.

Even though the arrow points down, the word *arrow* has to be lifted to draw attention to it.

Move the cursor until it is over the arrow

Stress either *move* or *cursor* but not both. Lift *over*.

and then click on the left mouse button.

Pause after *then*. Drop slightly on *button* as this is the end of the instructions in this extract.

You will now be able to see a list of the different places that you can save your document.

Lift *see* slightly and give the whole line a feeling of coming to a conclusion.

THE BIG BANGER – A Rap Script

Rap is everywhere and is often to be found in commercials. Authentic rap commercials are likely to be performed by authentic rappers. This is a rap written to publicise the Firework Safety Code and is part of a continuing radio and TV awareness campaign. It is aimed at children and young people and consequently the clarity of the words is more important than the authenticity of the performance.

Oh I'm the Big Banger and I'm all right
'Cos I know what to do on bonfire night.
Follow, follow, follow the firework code.
Now to help you all, I'm a useful chap,
So I've put together a safety rap.
Are you ready? Are you steady?
Let's go with the firework code.
Keep all your fireworks in a closed box
Read the instructions – there'll be no shocks
Light the fuse away from your face
Then stand well back from the firework place
Don't return when a firework's lit
Leave it alone – keep away from it
Never throw 'em or put 'em in your pocket
It's good advice and don't you knock it
Pets don't like the noise they make

So keep 'em indoors for safety's sake
Now here's the big one the final word
It's the wisest thing you've ever heard
Never Fool with Fireworks.

Who and Where?
You are the Big Banger – a street wise, bigtime firework. You know the score! Others don't dis you. You get maximum respect. You are leaping about a safe distance away from the bonfire demonstrating the finer points of the firework safety code.

What am I saying?
You are saying that it is cool to be safe.

When am I saying it?
At a firework party.

When is it going to be broadcast/transmitted?
Daytimes and early evenings.

Why am I saying it?
To entertain and educate children and young people.

How am I saying it?
In an appropriate rap or cartoon voice.

This script either has to be taught on a one to one basis or copied from an existing performance. There is a complete performance on the CD, as well as the backing track on its own. Rap along to the existing performance before trying it as a solo performance against the backing. The timing has to be spot on – the words and the music are as completely integrated as they would be in a song. When this is recorded it is done so as a series of drop-ins rather than as one complete performance.

INTERGALACTIC FEDERATION – A Computer Game

One large area of CD Rom work is computer games, although these draw more on the skills of the radio actor than the voice-over artist. Strong fantasy characterisations are required together with the ability to maintain the character. In order to conserve memory space the script will be recorded in as few sentences as possible so recurring phrases may well be recorded only once, with different inflections on the last word to cover both triumph and disaster.

These are then 'mixed and matched' by the host computer. It is important to ensure consistency of voice and accent so that they do 'match'!

By the standard of computer games the following is a long speech.

Welcome, Citizen to the Intergalactic Federation Information Disc. You are invited to join me on a brief tour of the interactive Gigazones.

The information to which you will be given access is of a highly sensitive nature, and I am pleased to inform you that you have been granted High Security Clearance for your journey.

However, before you leave the Gigazone, your cerebral cortex will be scanned and all sensitive information will be deleted. This is to safeguard Intergalactic Security. You must agree to this procedure before beginning your tour.

SFX

Thank you Citizen. Have a good journey.

Who and Where?

You are the villainous controller against whom the player pits his or her wits. You inhabit The Control Zone – a high tech area from which the empire can be surveyed and controlled. A suitable effects track is provided on the CD.

What am I saying?

You are disguising a command as an invitation. You are enticing the player into a catch 22 situation – if they take the tour they will not remember it, so what proof is there that they took it?

When am I saying it?

No specific time.

When is it going to be broadcast/transmitted?

It is part of a game so the character will appear whenever the game is played.

Why am I saying it?

To entice the player into your evil clutches.

How am I saying it?

You consider yourself to be infinitely superior to all mere mortals and you use politeness and good manners as offensive weapons. You are icily contemptuous.

Welcome, Citizen

This is said very precisely and coldly. Pause before *Citizen* and say it with an icy smile – make it sound like a term of abuse.

to the Intergalactic Federation Information Disc.

Use precise diction with a sense of pride. *Intergalactic Federation Information Disc* should all be at the same pitch.

You are invited

This is not an invitation – it is a command and should sound like an offer not to be refused.

to join me

Emphasise and lift *me*.

on a brief tour of the interactive Gigazones.

Keep the diction precise and lift and place *interactive Gigazones*.

The information to which you will be given access

Lift *information*, pause, then lift *access*.

is of a highly sensitive nature,

Sound a little cunning – as if you find it hard not to be gleeful at the impending trap.

and I am pleased to inform you

Pause slightly after *pleased* and then emphasise *you* by pointing.

that you have been granted

Lead towards and emphasise *granted*.

High Security Clearance for your journey.

Keep *High Security Clearance* up and pause at the end of it. Sound a little cunning during *for your journey*.

However,

Make it sound like the catch it is.

before you leave the Gigazone,

The emphasis is on *leave*.

your cerebral cortex will be scanned

Sound very pleased about this and keep *scanned* up.

and all sensitive information will be deleted.

Lift *sensitive information* and pause significantly before *deleted*.

This is to safeguard Intergalactic Security.

Make this sound terribly reasonable.

You must agree to this procedure before beginning your tour.

Suppressed gleeful triumph, with a pause after *procedure*. Emphasise *before* and lift *tour* in the expectation of a response.

SFX

A burbling sound effect that signifies that you have pressed the assent button on your control panel.

Thank you Citizen. Have a good journey.

Say *Thank you Citizen* very unctuously. *Have a good journey* must be politely triumphant. Pause after *good to* give it extra malevolence.

CONTINUITY SCRIPT – For Linking Broadcast Programmes

Continuity scripts used to be rather formal in style. The formality is now mixed with a lighter more entertaining approach. Certain news items – the death of a monarch for example – can only be broadcast in the most formal of tones and such announcements will only be made by the senior announcer of each network. Consequently, the dignity of the senior announcer is preserved; he or she would not be involved in the more zany links and trails. All radio and TV stations have permanent staff who can be assigned to this work. Announcers are expected to have scriptwriting abilities. Radio and TV stations also use outsiders on a freelance basis and some voices can be heard on two or more competing stations. The BBC employ full-time producers who devise and direct on-air publicity – they are responsible for employing outside artists and will listen to the tapes sent to them.

Continuity announcers can find themselves working under great pressure. The work is nearly always done live – what you say goes out on air as you say it – and as such has to be precisely timed. The weather forecast has finished 24 seconds earlier than expected. You were prepared to fill a 15-second spot and that has now more than doubled in length to 39 seconds. At the end of 39 seconds there will be the time signal. It is not permissible to 'crash' it. It will automatically be broadcast whether you have finished or not. You might have to make something up as you go along or you might have a few prepared scripts to cover such eventualities.

If you apply for a continuity or announcing job you will be asked to submit a tape before being considered for interview or audition.

This is the kind of script you would be expected to write and record. The running time is one minute! There are five announcements and the styles change between each. They cover a range of different approaches, from the light to the serious.

Wildlife on One – The Alien Empire – a fascinating glimpse into the lives of insects. Tonight – replicators – multiplication with a difference.

And now, Silent Witness, the start of a new eight-part Drama Series starring Amanda Burton. We would like to point out that this opening episode contains strong language and scenes which some viewers may find disturbing.

Jenny Hull and Eamonn Holmes answer some of those questions with the less than obvious answers in How Do They Do That?

This is BBC1. As you may have realised our programmes are running slightly later than advertised. This was caused by extra time being played in tonight's football match. And now – Question Time – which tonight comes from the studio in London. The Chairman is David Dimbleby.

It's Sunday evening and its time to dust down the contents of the attic as Hugh Scully introduces another edition of The Antiques Roadshow which tonight comes from Lymehall, in Cheshire.

Who and Where?
An unseen voice in the studio

What am I saying?
It varies but always contains information useful to the listener.

When am I saying it?
During breaks between programmes. Continuity announcements are made live – they are not pre-recorded.

When is it going to be broadcast/transmitted?
At any time.

Why am I saying it?
The reasons vary, from filling in a longer than expected break between programmes to explaining why the listener or viewer is not able to see the programme they were expecting. The main reason for on-air announcements is to retain listeners – to stop them from either switching off or changing channels.

How am I saying it?

It varies according to what you are saying.

Wildlife on One

This is a very popular programme and part of mainstream entertainment. The programme title, *Wildlife on One*, should be very 'up' and said with a modicum of pride.

The Alien Empire – a fascinating glimpse into the lives of insects

This is the title of the series within the overall programme name and a brief description of the content of the series.

Tonight – replicators – multiplication with a difference.

The announcement now becomes specific to the particular programme to be shown. *Replicators* needs to be lifted and the final four words should be said in a way which intrigues the listener enough to keep them watching.

And now, Silent Witness,

This is obviously a follow on from a 'That was' announcement. This is a 'serious' piece.

the start of a new eight-part Drama Series starring Amanda Burton.

Diction has to be very clear for the words *eight-part Drama Series* to make the 't' and the 'd' clear. The name of the star has to be lifted, but not too much because it is followed by a serious announcement.

We would like to point out that this opening episode contains strong language and scenes which some viewers may find disturbing.

Pause after *out* and *episode*. Lift *language* and *disturbing* slightly.

Jenny Hull and Eamonn Holmes answer some of those questions with the less than obvious answers in

This is light-hearted so both stars' names need to be lifted and smiled through at the beginning. Pause after *questions* and be slightly enigmatic over *with the less than obvious answers. Less* and *answers* need to be emphasised by lifting the pitch. Pause after *answers* and lift and isolate *in.*

How Do They Do That?

Never mind how they do it – how do you say it? On the page these five words seem easy enough. The difficulty arises when you say them out loud. There are an astonishing number of ways of inflecting the phrase and consequently a large number of very different meanings. The safest choice is to emphasise the first and last words.

This is BBC1.

Emphasise *this* and lift *BBC1.*

As you may have realised our programmes are running slightly later than advertised.

This needs a slightly apologetic tone. Pause after *realised.*

This was caused by extra time being played in tonight's football match.

Lift *extra time* and *football match.* Say the whole sentence as one phrase without a break or breath.

And now – Question Time – which tonight comes from the studio in London.

This is a serious discussion programme so do not introduce it as though it were a circus act. Slightly lift *tonight* and pause afterwards because the programme comes from a different location every week.

The Chairman is David Dimbleby.

It always is, but lift *David Dimbleby* nevertheless.

It's Sunday evening and its time to dust down the contents of the attic

This is light-hearted, so smile and say it with a degree of physical animation.

as Hugh Scully introduces another edition of The Antiques Roadshow

Lift *Hugh Scully* and then lift *The Antiques Roadshow.*

which tonight comes from Lymehall, in Cheshire.

Observe the comma after *Lymehall.* Do not go down on *Cheshire.*

SPORTS TRAILER

Sports commentaries are a law unto themselves and very much subject to fashion – you can come across voices from all classes and cultures. Some, like horse racing commentators, whip themselves into a frenzy, while snooker, pool and billiards games are described in the hushed tones more often associated with wildlife commentaries. This is a 30-second radio script advertising the weekend's events on Sport FM. The music used can be found on the CD. The script starts after the high note of the opening fanfare.

Tonight 7.30. Full 90 minutes commentary. England versus Germany on 108.5 Sport FM. Your big match presenter – Richard Striker.

Saturday 1pm, a full five hours of the very best sports coverage in the country: motor racing from France, rugby union from Twickenham, cricket live from South Africa – plus – Full results service, half time scores and racing results.

108.5 Sport FM – The number one sports station.

Who and Where?
You are a studio voice.

What am I saying?
As well as giving details of specific events you are telling the (already converted listeners) how good the sports coverage is on Sport FM.

When am I saying it?
No specific time.

When is it going to be broadcast/transmitted?
Throughout the day and night.

Why am I saying it?
To ensure that the station keeps its audience.

How am I saying it?
With a great deal of energy but not volume. The voice used has to be genuine and not assumed. Most voices are acceptable, but it has to be said that the script is unlikely to be delivered in the most cultured of tones.

Tonight 7.30

The first word needs to be explosive but clear. The clenched fist with the pointing finger should give the right feel. *7.30* should be a little higher in pitch than *tonight*.

Full 90 minutes commentary. England versus Germany

The first half – *Full 90 minutes commentary* – is best delivered on one note, almost song-like. *England versus Germany* needs a gradually ascending pitch throughout.

on 108.5 Sport FM.

This is the all-important station identification and you need to be very clear how you are going to phrase it – it has to sound confident. The frequency is said as 'one oh eight point five' with an upward

feel, while *Sport FM* has a lower pitch. Try nodding as you say it –
it creates a sporting intimacy between you and the listener.

Your big match presenter Richard Striker.

The first four words need to end on a raised pitch, while *Richard Striker* is dropped in pitch but not energy.

Saturday 1pm,

The whole script goes up an excitement notch at this point as a way of keeping the listener's attention. *Saturday* and *1pm* should be separated, with *1pm* at a higher pitch.

a full five hours of the very best sports coverage in the country:

Five hours should be emphasised, but the whole line needs the feeling of being sung on or around one note.

motor racing from France,

See it and point to it – keep the delivery quite staccato.

rugby union from Twickenham,

See it and point to it in a different place.

cricket live from South Africa

In this line the word *live* is functioning as an added value word so it needs lifting and isolating.

– plus – Full results service, half time scores

Another added value word – *plus*. Point to *Full results service,* and *half time scores.*

and racing results.

The third added value word in quick succession. *Racing results* must be up.

108.5 Sport FM – The number one sports station.

The station identity is the same as earlier in the script. *The number one sports station* can be said any number of ways, with many different inflections and pauses. It is a matter of making a decision and then sounding confident.

VOICE PROMPT SYSTEMS

This is a growing area of work.

The automated systems now being used by Directory Enquiry services include wonderful examples of bad inflections and bad joins. The announcement: *The number you requested is,* always flows very well because it was recorded as a complete phrase. However, the numbers which follow can be so disjointed that they sound as if they were recorded by someone who was shaken violently every time they opened their mouth.

Telephone number systems created by recording all numbers and instructions only once each invariably sound strange. A computer can string all the numbers and announcements together to meet all possible combinations but they will probably not be memorable and thereby defeat the purpose of the system.

One suggestion that the voice-over artist could make would be to record *double one, double two, double three,* etc. as complete phrases rather than letting the computer find the words *double* and *five* and stringing them together. It is a good idea to record each individual digit twice – once for use at the start of, or within, a number, and once for use at the end of a number. The inflections are entirely different.

This is a typical script for an automated answering system. A company looking for a voice for a new system will only want to hear something appropriate. There is no point sending them poetry, prose or commercials.

Thank you for calling
If you require Sales or Enquiries, please press 1.
Sales for customers whose company name begins with letters
A to E – press 1,
from F to O – press 2,
and from P to Z – press 3.
If you require an extension number directly, please press 2
and the extension number required, followed by hash
If you require technical support, please press 3.
If you require printing materials, please press 4.
If you do not have a star or hash sign on your phone please
hold the line and you will be answered shortly.

Thank you for calling – I'm sorry the office is closed.

If you would like to be connected directly to an extension,
please press 2 and the extension number required.
If you do not have a direct extension number, please hold and
you will be answered shortly – if someone is available.
If there is no one available, please leave a message and we
will return your call.

Telephone prompts are usually female. The theory is that men enjoy listening to a well-modulated female voice and women do not object to being given instructions (please press 2, etc.), by another woman. The style of delivery has to be friendly but not too informal. Falling inflections sound depressed and present the company in an unfortunate light. The script requires gently rising inflections because one prompt inevitably leads to another and the system may jump to any line in the script depending on which numbers have been pressed by the caller. There is a recording of this script on the CD.

CHILDREN'S WORK – The Dragon Who Couldn't Help Breathing Fire

Children's stories rank alongside wildlife documentaries as a 'must do' area of work for people entering the profession. Most children's tapes are bought by adults for children. Adults like to see a familiar name on the label so, unfortunately, this work is mostly given to 'stars' – whether or not they are any good at it! Fees in this area can be very low because the shop buyers insist on huge profit margins (as much as 50 per cent) and low selling prices – £1 (less than $2.00) is not an uncommon price. However, newcomers do find employment from time to time. There may be opportunities on local radio stations or with tape companies that are just starting up. This is an extract from a delightful story about a dragon. There is suitable opening and closing music on the CD.

> The tearful dragon decided to go home. He knew he'd never find a friend, because he just couldn't help breathing fire.
> On the way to his cave, he passed a small cottage.
> 'Hello!' he heard a voice call, and a little old woman hurried from the cottage towards him.
> 'Don't come too near,' he warned her, kindly. 'I'm a dragon. I breathe fire!'
> 'I don't care if you're a monster from outer space,' said the little old woman, 'just so long as you can help me.'
> And she pulled the dragon through her cottage door.
> 'My stove has gone out,' explained the little old woman, 'and I can't cook my dinner.'
> 'I can light it for you,' said the dragon. 'But you'll have to make me laugh!'
> The little old woman popped a saucepan on her head and danced a very funny dance around the kitchen. But it wasn't funny enough to make the dragon laugh. She cart-wheeled across the room, singing silly songs and pulling silly faces. But still she couldn't make the dragon laugh.
> Then she had an idea. She grabbed her feather duster and tickled under the dragon's arm. The dragon roared with

laughter. He was very ticklish. With the flames that shot from his mouth, the dragon lit the old woman's stove.

'Would you like to stay for dinner?' she asked. 'There's plenty here for two.'

The dinner was delicious, and both the dragon and the little old woman had plenty to talk about.

'Will you come and see me again tomorrow?' asked the little old woman.

A very happy dragon climbed into bed that night.

'I've found a friend,' he chuckled.

And as he did so, a tiny flame oozed from the corner of his mouth.

This script requires 3 voices – the narrator, the dragon, and the little old lady.

You are the narrator – the storyteller. Do not be condescending in the 'Once upon a time' tradition as children find it boring. 'Once upon a time' is not boring in itself – it is the sickly 'Let's talk to children' voice which so often says it that's boring! Narrators must remember to smile, to keep an upward inflection, and to enjoy the story.

The dragon is slightly morose because he scares everyone away by breathing fire when he laughs and, try as he can, he can't help finding the world a very funny place. English north country is a very good accent for dragons.

The little old lady is very spry and not at all afraid of dragons – she is quite happy to dance around the kitchen with a saucepan on her head. A Scottish accent would suit her very well.

It is important to use the accents only when the character is speaking and to drop it for the 'he said, she said' sections.

7

The Studio

Most voice-overs are performed and recorded in a 'recording studio', although I have also known them to be recorded in cupboards, corridors, hotel bedrooms, washrooms, and even cars! Many are now recorded over ISDN lines, with the performer at home in the cupboard under the stairs, in the garden shed, or in the cellar. Some are even recorded from ordinary domestic telephones. These are usually for companies who are themselves disseminating information over the telephone system – banks, consumer groups, weather and traffic conditions, ticket sales, and sports reports.

Voice artists are not expected to understand how a studio works, but a general understanding of the principles and practice of recording will make for a better relationship with the studio engineer. The level of knowledge required is rather like that needed to drive a car. You can learn how to drive a car without knowing how it works. However, if you have some understanding of its internal mechanisms you can become a much better driver. Some television and radio continuity suites are designed to be operated by the voice-over without the aid of an engineer. There are known as 'self-op' studios. They are not technically complicated and may require nothing more difficult than flicking a power switch and setting a volume level for the microphone. Anyone investing in an ISDN line and the associated equipment will need to know how to use it without knowing how it actually works.

Some recording studios are astonishingly hi-tech, with those that specialise in music recording looking more futuristic in terms of both equipment and decor than the Starship Enterprise! The operation of a modern studio is often referred to as 'driving'. The largest and most comfortable chair in any studio is inevitably occupied by the engineer who operates the recording equipment. Its size and comfort reflect not only the long hours he may spend seated at the controls, but also the immense electronic power at his disposal. This seat and these controls are the engineer's domain; do not touch either of them unless specifically invited to do so.

All that is required to record a technically acceptable voice-over is a good microphone and a high quality recording machine. Early machines which recorded onto wire, tape or wax discs were noisy. To prevent this noise from being picked up by the microphone the machines were housed in a small, slightly soundproofed room built into one corner of the studio. This was referred to as the 'cubicle', a term still used by the BBC today. The voice-over artist occupied a much larger space than the engineer. If you listen to recordings made before about 1960, the voices sound as if they were recorded in large reverberant rooms. You will also notice that the voices are quite loud – the actors are not shouting but they are certainly using stage projection techniques. Diction was very formal and clipped and the whole feel was always of 'addressing the Nation'. BBC radio always insisted that radio announcers and newsreaders (newscasters) wore formal evening dress. Modern voice-over artists and announcers now only address themselves to 'one' person so the delivery and the recording or broadcasting environment are more intimate and cosy. Microphones are much more sensitive and can pick up the quietest of voices. The modern style is more the friend next to you rather than the headmaster from the stage. 'Schooltalk' has become 'pillowtalk'!

As the style of delivery has changed, so the layout of the studio and the amount of equipment required have also changed. In fact, the situation has been completely reversed. The voice artist now occupies the smaller space – known as the 'booth'. The engineer and the equipment have expanded to fill the larger space – known as the 'control room'.

THE BOOTH

The voice-over booth is where the voice-over artist sits or stands to make the recording. They can vary in size from being large enough to accommodate only one person at a time to those designed for two or three people. Some are bought as prefabricated units, while others are converted cupboards or rooms in the building housing the studio. The booth has two main functions: it has to provide an acoustically dead environment free of the echoes and reverberations of a normal room, and it has to exclude the sounds of the outside world. These can be the noises of the recording machines, the chatter of clients, ringing telephones, and the sounds of passing traffic, aeroplanes, trains, and underground (subway) trains. The booth may have air conditioning or air extraction – or it may not! Modern microphones are so sensitive that they will easily pick up the sounds made by these systems. If the script being recorded is accompanied by music or sound effects, these will probably mask the noise. If a talking book is being recorded without music or sound effects, then any air conditioning or extraction will have to remain switched off during recording time.

Booths can get hot so it is wise to wear thin layers of clothing which can be easily removed and replaced. Because the microphones are so sensitive they can pick up the sounds made by clothing, jewellery and watches. Wear clothes made from silent fabrics: cotton is quiet but leather is noisy. Remove all dangling or hanging jewellery, and if you have a watch which ticks noisily leave it in the control room. Remember to switch off mobile telephones and audible pagers.

Noisy mouths and rumbling stomachs can be a problem. Sipping from a glass of water will help to silence a sticky palate, and lip salve or Vaseline should alleviate smacking lips. Small quantities of food – biscuits, for example – can quell the rumbling tummy. If you know that you suffer from any of these conditions it would be wise to keep food and still (non-gassy) water with you. Avoid studio coffee as it can cause more problems than it solves.

It is considered good and considerate practice not to wear perfume, aftershave or anything else that smells strongly. Perfume and aftershave evaporate more quickly in the warm conditions of the studio, and the smell in the booth can soon become offensive. You may be working with someone who is allergic to certain fragrances and your perfume might cause them to sneeze or wheeze. Most voice artists avoid eating garlic for about 24 hours before a session in which they will be working closely with others. It may also be wise to refrain from eating foods which cause flatulence. People will not say anything to you if you do go to the studio smelling of perfume or garlic – they will simply make a note not to book you for any future work. Remember that your sole aim during one session is to get booked for the next.

The booth will probably contain a chair and a table which is covered with a thick, soft material, usually felt, to deaden the sound of the script and to stop any sound being reflected off the shiny wooden surface underneath. There may be a small stand on which to put the script and there should also be a jug of water and a glass. Everything is arranged so that you can go into the booth and sit down in comfort. However, you would be much better off standing! Sitting is very good for the engineer but not good for you or your performance. Sitting constricts the diaphragm, encourages bad posture, and effectively stops you from using half of your body. Stand up and be 'on your toes'. Your stance can change your voice. Your body language should come through loud and clear. You need to be as animated as the script requires.

Try not to arrive at the studio wearing inappropriate footwear. High-heeled shoes or thick-soled stamping boots have no place in the sound studio. You should be very grounded and in touch with your surroundings, and the wrong shoes can insulate you from your environment. Many voice artists prefer to work in bare feet. One of the basic tenets of T'ai Chi is very applicable to the voice-over field: 'Stand like a mountain, flow like a river'.

You can either hold the script, usually in the left hand, or you can put it on a music stand. However, if you are booked for five days to record a talking book you really have no choice – sitting is the sensible option.

Headphones

The booth should also contain a set of headphones, known as 'cans'. Headphones are a basic tool of the trade. There are four main reasons for wearing them.

(1) When in the booth it is not possible to hear what is being said in the control room. If the engineer or producer want to talk to you they press the 'talkback' button and their voices are routed to your cans. If they do not press the talkback button you cannot hear them, and if you do not wear the cans all you will hear is a tiny disembodied voice which will probably be saying, 'Put the cans on, please'!

(2) If you are working with music, sound effects, or another voice artist being patched-in from a remote studio, the only way you will be able to hear them is through the cans.

(3) You can ask for your voice to be routed to your cans and this allows you to hear it at a greater volume than that at which it is transmitted to your ears through the bones of your head. In other words, you can hear exactly what the microphone hears. This should allow you to treat your voice like an instrument and have more control over it. It can be a shock when you hear your own voice picked up by a superb mic and relayed at quite a high volume to your ears. Having your own voice in your ears can be quite addictive and most people become completely dependent on it very quickly and are unable to work without it.

(4) Wearing headphones allows you to do a 'drop-in'. Scripts used to have to be recorded in one 'take', starting at the beginning and proceeding faultlessly to the end. Any mistakes meant starting again. Consequently, voice artists tended to play safe. When magnetic tape became commonplace, various sections of several takes were spliced together to make one good take. With modern recording equipment it is possible to replay the recording up to an agreed point in the script whereupon the machine instantly switches from replay to record and the voice artist continues. This method of editing is known as doing a 'drop-in', a term borrowed from the world of rock 'n roll recording. It is a skill that has to be

practised – a bad drop-in is very noticeable. The trick is to read out loud along with the part of the script that you hear in the headphones just before the drop-in point. Your initial reading will not be recorded, but when the machine switches from play to record the energy of your reading will be at the appropriate level. If you do not do this 'reading along' you will probably start the section you are replacing with the energy of a 'start' rather than a 'continuation'. With practice and experience it is quite possible to drop-in at any point in a script, and sometimes it is possible to drop just one word into the middle of a sentence, provided, of course, that you are working with a skilled engineer.

When you walk into the booth one of the most 'professional' things that you can do is to put the headphones on – or at the very least put them around your neck. If you do put them around your neck you will easily hear if someone is trying to talk to you and you can then put them over your ears.

The headphones used in studios are usually the 'closed' type. This means that when you are wearing them none of the sound you are listening to escapes and is picked up by the mic. If you listen to a voice track recorded when the artist is wearing 'open' headphones you will also hear the trebly sound of the music or FX track being relayed to the voice artist. This sounds exactly like the sound you hear when someone on the train or bus is listening to their Walkman. If the music or FX track is subsequently not used or changed, the voice recording becomes unusable because of the 'spill' from the original track.

Some people insist on wearing their cans with one ear on and one ear off. This, like all compromises, is not entirely satisfactory. The headphone of the 'off' ear can leak sound which is then picked up by the microphone, thus rendering the voice track useless if the backing tracks are changed or scrapped. It is best to get used to wearing headphones and avoid the reputation of being 'difficult'. Only when you get to the stage where 'they' need you more than you need them can you afford to have 'difficult' tag attached to your name.

The engineer has complete control over the sounds being fed to your headphones, and you can ask him to adjust them to your liking. Standard practice is for you to read from the script while the engineer increases the volume of your voice in the headphones from complete silence up to the point where you say 'fine'. He will then bring in the music and FX until you are happy with the relative levels. If necessary you can ask for the levels to be changed as the session progresses. Sounds relayed to you in your cans are known as 'foldback'.

Be careful where you put the headphones when you take them off; do not put them on or near the microphone. If the engineer has not switched off the mic, 'feedback' can occur between the two. The microphone picks up the headphones, which are listening to the microphone, which is picking up the headphones . . . This generates a high-pitched whistle which, if not stopped, increases in volume until something in the signal chain is destroyed. It is very painful to listen to and can permanently damage hearing. BBC engineers traditionally refer to feedback as howlround – a far more descriptive term.

Foldback

The booth may also contain one or two foldback speakers. These may be used to replay your recording to you. This is known as playback. Headphones have a limited frequency response and you can better evaluate your performance by listening to playback on loud speakers. If you decide not to wear headphones the engineer might be able to route the talkback circuit to the foldback speakers. He will not be able to route the foldback of your voice to these speakers as this would cause feedback when recording. He is also unable to play the music or FX track via the foldback speakers as this would spill on to the voice track. It is important to have a clear understanding of the four 'backs' – talk, fold, play and feed!

The booth may contain a cue light which will be used to give you your 'cue'. The BBC uses a red light to tell you when to start. Most independent studios use a green light, and in some 'digital' studios you will hear a short electronic tone in the headphones. Recordings made in theatre recording studios will often give you a red light to stand-by followed 30 seconds later by a green light to start.

There may be a silent clock with a second hand which can be very useful when doing commercial scripts that have to be read in a specific number of seconds. If you are synchronising speech to pictures there will be a video monitor.

As well as audio links with the control room, the booth may have visual communication. Some booths contain a video camera which relays a picture of the voice artist to a video monitor in the control room. It is very rare for the control room to contain a camera relaying pictures to the artist in the booth. Most booths have a window giving direct line of sight communication with the control room. They can see you, and you can see them. They can hear you because your mic is on but you can only hear them when they deign to press the talkback button. This situation – known as the 'fishtank effect' – conspires to generate paranoia and insecurity in the voice artist. You will be able to see 'them' in deep and meaningful conversation and, because you cannot hear what they are saying, you are tempted to imagine that they are discussing your shortcomings and the swiftest (and cheapest) way of dispensing with your services. This is never the case. They are more likely to be discussing last night's sport or television. However, your mic is probably always 'live' and anything you say, mutter under your breath, or any noisy bodily function will be clearly audible in the control room. For all you know it may be recorded as well!

Microphones

The booth will always contain at least one microphone and stand. Voice-over microphones are usually much larger than the microphones used to record instruments. Instrument mics often pick up sound from one direction only so that they can be pointed at a specific instrument without picking up the sound of others. Voice-over mics are large and are designed to pick up sound in a heart-shaped pattern in front of them. They contain a large gold-plated diaphragm which converts the sound waves into electrical impulses. This diaphragm is both sensitive and delicate and you should never sneeze, blow or cough into the mic. You should also never tap the mic or attempt to move it. If you move such a sensitive mic when it is 'on', the sound level generated could be enough to damage the monitor speakers and cause great discomfort to anyone listening in the control room. If you want the mic moved, ask the engineer or his assistant to do it for you – studio equipment is very expensive! A good voice-over mic costs at least £1,000 ($1,600). The most popular mic is the Neuman U87 which, including the special suspension cradle, costs about £2,000 ($3,200).

Microphone Technique

If knowing what to do with the headphones is one sign of the professional then correct microphone technique is another. The distance between yourself and the microphone is critical. Maintaining that distance is even more critical! Voice-over microphones are designed to exploit the 'proximity effect'. The microphone picks up extra bass frequencies as the speaker gets closer to it.

Bass sounds can travel far greater distances than sounds in other parts of the audio spectrum. Whales and elephants use very low frequencies (many of them below our lower hearing threshold) to communicate over vast distances. The only sounds we hear from the overloud distant party or concert are the bass notes of the music. Because we can hear only the bass frequencies we know that the sound is coming from a great distance, although we may find it difficult to know from which direction the sound is coming since bass frequencies do not carry any directional information. Position is determined by listening in stereo (we have two ears) to the high frequency sounds. Modern cinema-sound home hi-fi systems have one bass speaker which can be placed anywhere, and two (left and right) speakers handling the mid- and high frequencies. Cinemas and film makers place great emphasis on accentuating the bass content of films. The highly exaggerated bass makes the action seem much closer.

The human body not only receives sound through the ears; Evelyn Glennie, the profoundly deaf percussionist, is able to perform to great critical acclaim because she 'hears' sound through her body. High frequency sounds are received by the face and low frequencies by the genitals. The whine of the old-fashioned dentist's drill was doubly painful because the sound of the instrument was being received by the very area on which it was likely to inflict pain. The scratching sound of chalk on a school blackboard is often complained of because it 'puts the teeth on edge'. Bass frequencies, being received by the genitals, are associated with pleasure. Record producers, discos and radio stations make sure that their bass sounds are as strong as possible – sex sells!

The voice-over mic accentuates the bass content of the voice and makes the speaker seem to be physically very close. This closeness is designed to make the listener feel as if the speaker is inside their personal space, while the sound of their voice is probably causing mild involuntary sexual arousal. Again 'schooltalk has become pillowtalk'! The speaker who used to address the masses on a formal basis now whispers to the individual with a surprising degree of intimacy.

A good mouth to mic distance can be found by placing the thumb of the outstretched hand on the end of the nose and touching the microphone with the little finger. Big people with big voices have bigger hands and so are further away from the mic than small people with smaller hands and voices. This rule of thumb is easy to remember and will ensure that you accurately reposition yourself at the mic after each recording break. It is very important to maintain a consistent mouth to mic distance as any variation will sound as if you are either getting closer to or further away from the listener. Either of these will detract from your message and probably annoy the listener.

Popping

Working this closely to the microphone is not without its dangers. You have to develop very good technical control of the voice. The big problem is 'popping'. This is where plosive consonants such as 'p' and 'b' are given too much energy and overload the diaphragm in the mic. This causes a popping or banging sound. The extra blast of air generated by these sounds can be seen by holding a sheet of A4 paper in front of the mouth and firing off a few energetic 'p's and 'b's. The paper will move noisily. The main cause of this problem is actors who use stage projection in front of the microphone. It is not necessary! On stage you address an audience that

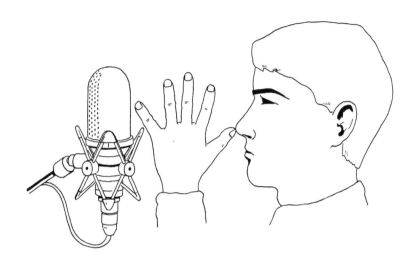

A fixed distance from the microphone.

can be anything up to 2,000 strong. It is necessary to ensure that your words are both heard and understood. In the voice-over booth your perceived audience is one, so there is no need either to project or shout. One way of dealing with the symptom, but not the cause, is to increase the mouth to mic distance until the diaphragm can cope with the extra blast of air caused by the plosives. This reduces the bass content in the voice, however, and so makes it sound more distant.

Another solution is to use a 'pop shield' – also known as a 'pop screen' or 'popper stopper'. This is usually a small screen covered with nylon which can be placed between the mouth and the mic to dissipate the unwanted air. It is not infallible, however. A pencil held in front of the lips when saying words containing plosives has a similar effect. It divides the blast of air and diverts it either side of the microphone. Other sounds such as 'th', 'f', and 's' can also cause problems if you breath out when saying them. 'Th' and 'f' can cause pops while 's' can become oversibilant (see next page). Rather than finding ways of dealing with the problem it is better to learn not to cause pops and not to be excessively sibilant.

THE CONTROL ROOM

The sound from the mic in the voice-over booth is fed into the control room where it is listened to on loudspeakers known as 'monitors'. There are usually at least two pairs of these. One is large and can be listened to at high volume to give an idea of what the recording might sound like in a cinema. The other pair is smaller and designed to sound like a first class hi-fi system. These smaller speakers are often referred to as 'nearfield' monitors. There may also be a pair of low cost speakers from a car radio as these approximate to the sound of the average portable system. The engineer ensures that your voice sounds good on all of these monitors.

Before the sound reaches the monitors and monitor amplifier it passes through the 'mixing' desk. This is usually in front of the engineer and consists of rows of knobs and faders (volume controls). These control the volume and tone of sounds passing through the desk. The engineer can increase or decrease the bass, mid-, and high frequency content of your voice. Desks can be either analogue or digital. Analogue is the more traditional, but the modern digital desks convert the electrical impulses from the mic (analogue) into digital information which is both easier to manipulate and process and easy to transmit over long distances. There is a move back to using analogue valve (tube) technology as it is thought to give a warmer sound to voice recordings. The recording and mixing desks of the 21st century are likely to combine the best elements of both old and new technology.

Effects And Processors

If your voice is too sibilant the engineer can pass the sound through a 'de-esser' which electronically removes most of the unwanted sound. The drawback is that it removes some of the wanted sound as well. Sibilance is the hissing that accompanies the 's' sound. It is caused by air passing over the teeth. The best cure is not to do it and to be aware of not breathing out through the 's' sound.

If you read a script at varying volumes – with some words louder or quieter than others – the mic may be routed to a 'compressor'. This piece of equipment is much beloved of recording engineers throughout the world. The best way to compensate for changes in 'level' is to move the microphone volume control up and down as the volume varies. This is known as riding the fader and requires a very skilled and patient engineer. The compressor is the electronic equivalent of the engineer's hand. If it is not used skilfully it has the disadvantage of making all the quiet sounds louder. This is most noticeable on breaths and can make you sound as if you are recording the script while running a marathon. If the compressor is set to compensate for only the loudest of sounds it is said to be acting as a limiter. It is best to develop a vocal technique which makes the use of a compressor or limiter unnecessary.

Compressors are sometimes deliberately used to give a feeling of barely suppressed energy to a recording. A 'ducking compressor' is set to reduce the volume of music or FX the instant you start speaking. Radio DJs usually use a ducking compressor. The compressor can be heard at its worst when used in tape machines recording the live news reports filed by journalists working for small independent radio stations. Every gap between words or sentences is filled by a huge surge in the background noise (usually traffic) which miraculously disappears the moment the journalist continues.

If you have been asked to read a script in 29 seconds but 31 is the best you can do, a piece of computer software called 'Timeline' can adjust the length of your read to fit the required time. This is achieved without raising the pitch of the recording.

If the pitch of your voice has to be raised or lowered to produce a sci-fi or comic effect it is usually done by a piece of equipment called a 'harmoniser'. This electronically raises or lowers the pitch of a recording without raising or lowering the speed.

Other effects which can be applied to the voice are 'echo' and 'reverb', which makes you sound as if you are speaking in a large hall. The two are sometimes combined.

Recording Formats

Once the sound has passed through the desk it is recorded. There are five main recording formats in use today.

(1) **Tape.** This is the traditional medium. It is very easy to edit as sections of tape can be physically cut up and spliced back together again to make one excellent take from a series of good ones. Many people prefer tape as a medium for voice recording as it gives a much warmer sound than digital which is thought to be slightly harsh. Tape can also be used for the final master recording.

(2) **Adat.** This is digital recording on SVHS video tape. Adat machines are eight-track – one Adat machine is the equivalent of four stereo tape recorders running in parallel. It makes it very easy to keep several takes and compare them with each other. Complicated editing requires two or more machines and the associated controller. The Adat system is very popular with music and voice studios as one SVHS tape can store eight hours of mono voice without taking up to much valuable shelf space.

(3) **Computer.** Systems such as Sadie and Pro-Tools are computer-based, with the recorded sound appearing as visual information on the monitor screen. It is very easy to manipulate sound within a computer – removing breaths, making composite recordings from

several takes, and editing words or parts of words are all relatively simple operations in the hands of a skilled engineer. It is easy to lose or wipe a recording since the information exists only within the memory of the computer. Computer recordings of voices are sometimes thought to sound rather harsh.

(4) **DAT.** Digital Audio Tape is now a universal format and all good studios will have a least one Dat machine. It is used as a mastering medium for storing the final mix. Completed recordings are often sent from one studio to another on Dat tapes. Each tape can store up to two hours of stereo sound at higher than CD quality and is not much larger than a box of matches. As it is so small it is easy to lose a Dat tape, so beware!

(5) **MiniDisc.** This is the consumer format available in all hi-fi stores. The discs are physically small but can store as much music or speech as a CD. The quality is not quite as high as a CD but in most cases the difference cannot be detected by the human ear. Some users prefer MiniDisc to CD or DAT because the player/recorders incorporate a few useful editing facilities.

Most studios can manufacture one-off CDs and these are used for storing and archiving material. They are also given to clients so that completed recordings can be evaluated in the domestic environment. They are the cheapest professional recording medium in use. Cassettes are cheaper but the quality of cassettes and cassette players is so variable that they are only used as a last resort. A cassette which sounds wonderful on one system may sound dreadful on another if the Dolby/Chrome Metal/Normal Loudness Treble/Bass/Bass Boost and Equaliser controls are in the wrong place.

Music and FX

Sound recording studios nearly always maintain a comprehensive library of sound effects discs and tapes. These are known as FX discs. They range from the sounds of the countryside to imaginative realisations of Martian swamp-monsters; anything imaginable is available or can be created. Hollywood film studios sell their FX libraries for commercial use and several excellent FX libraries are available for audition and downloading over the Internet. All you need is a credit or charge card.

Most studios have a large selection of production music, also known as library music. This is specially created for media use and is not available to the general public. Each disc deals with a theme or genre. Among the obvious categories are sport, industry, wildlife, space travel, comedy, children, and large quantities of music classified by geographical or cultural origin. Music created for

127

advertising uses exists in the standard lengths of 9½, 19½, 29½, 39½, and 59½ seconds.

When recording a commercial or commentary, music and FX may be played to you over the foldback circuit to generate a mood or feeling. You can always ask for this if you feel that it would help your performance. This may or may not be used in the final mix. It might be replaced by music specially commissioned to blend with your voice and phrasing.

8

Making Your Own Tape

Making a voice tape is a big and significant step; if you do not make the right decisions it can be an expensive business. There is a booming industry growing up around the making of tapes on both sides of the Atlantic. The cost ranges from $4,000 (£2,700) in Los Angeles to as low as £75 ($120) in London. The waters in between these two cities and prices are infested with sharks eager to take your money. The most expensive is not necessarily the best, and the cheapest is not necessarily the worst. It is very important to talk to voice people and find out who they go to for their tapes. You will find that two sets of names keep recurring – the good and the bad. Both have reputations; avoid the one and embrace the other. The bad person has nothing to lose by ripping off yet another sucker and will do so without compunction. The good person has everything to lose and would rather refuse to take your money than do a bad job. A good voice tape producer will be choosy about the people they agree to work with. Money alone will not buy their services – you will have to convince them that you are worthy of their attention.

Without a tape you are very unlikely to even be considered for work by potential employers. If you submit a home-made tape you will be promoting yourself as an amateur, and who wants to entrust their beloved script to someone without experience? Your tape is your calling card, your trade sample, and the key to opening the doors of the voice-over world. It has to be recorded, produced and packaged to the highest possible standard.

COWBOYS

There are several warning signs that should alert you to the unscrupulous operator:

- avoid anyone who suggests that you write your own commercials or commentaries. They do not know what they are talking about.

You want to be a voice artist not a scriptwriter. The two professions are entirely different and there is very little, if any, cross fertilisation between the two. It is the job of the producer to provide you with suitable, authentic material. A potential employer will want to hear you reading known, recognisable scripts. Faked commercials are instantly obvious to professionals within the advertising world. Spoof commercials which satirise the real world of advertising guarantee that your tape will be thrown in the bin after five seconds. It's those first five seconds that get (or lose) you the job! Advertising agencies often play voice artists' tapes to their clients for initial approval or assessment. How can they play something that does not take the business of advertising seriously? One extraordinary example which I heard recently extolled the virtues of 'Tampax for Men'! If this had been for a First Aid infomercial dealing with unstoppable nosebleeds it might have been acceptable! But it wasn't.

- avoid anyone who suggests that you take group classes in voice-over during the course of which 'we all go into the studio and make our tapes'. Learning voice-over is an intensely private and personal affair. You do not need an audience when experimenting with differing voices and reads. The presence of other people will make you very self-conscious. If you all go to the studio together how much individual time are you going to get? I started group classes in London in the early 1980s and I discontinued them after one course because they did not work well for the students. The only effective way to work is in a studio on a one to one basis. Try to find a producer with his own studio who can simultaneously engineer, produce, teach and direct – and who does not charge £2000!

- avoid anyone who tells you how good they themselves are at voice-overs and what a wonderful career they have. If it is so wonderful why are they interested in teaching you? The puppet does not necessarily know how the strings are pulled! Put yourself in the hands of the puppet master, not the puppet!

- avoid anyone who gives you the hard sell to get you sign up for a class or studio session. A good producer will have a waiting list and will not need to put any pressure on you.

- avoid anyone who advertises outside of the 'professional' papers. You should only put yourself in the hands of producers who deal with professionals. Good producers hardly need to advertise – they will probably only be listed in trade directories. The majority of their business will come from the recommendations of satisfied clients.

- avoid anyone who tells you what a wonderful voice you have and how much money you will make – if only you come to them for a demo!

CLASSES

If you do feel the need for classes it is better to go to one of the recognised training organisations and take lessons in sight reading, diction, interpretation, radio acting, or even voice-over. By attending established classes you will meet other people who share your interests. You will begin to feel part of the voice-over world. You can exchange information about voice tape producers, potential employers, possible agents, and other useful contacts in the voice world.

FINDING A STUDIO

If you choose not to put yourself in the hands of a reputable producer you will have to find a studio in which to record. It is not possible to make a professional sounding tape on domestic equipment; there is no comparison between the ordinary hi-fi microphones and the ones used in voice-over studios. Many musicians have four- or eight-track recording machines which they use for making music demos, but these are not suitable for voice work as they do not usually accept voice-over mics. Any voice recording that is done in a bedroom or sitting room will have the wrong 'acoustic': the sounds of the ticking clock, passing traffic and neighbouring children will detract from the credibility of your work.

Commercial studios can be found by looking in Yellow Pages. Some advertise on noticeboards in music shops and in music and showbusiness publications. Local branches of performers' unions and associations may be able to make recommendations. Advertising Agencies might tell you where they record their commercials and some local radio stations hire out their commercial production facilities for evening sessions. Some schools, colleges and universities have very sophisticated sound studios and it may be possible to hire one of these. However, you will need the services of their resident engineer as it would be unwise to put yourself in the hands of a student!

Choosing which studio to use can be difficult. The best course of action is to find one that already records voices and commercials because they will know exactly how to make you sound professional. See if you can afford their hourly rates. If they are too expensive for you try offering some money and some payment in kind. Perhaps you could do some voice recording free of charge, or do a day's work in their office. Using a studio which already works in the voice market can have other benefits – if they like you they may be able to suggest useful contacts for you, or they may even be able to use you themselves.

Studios record either speech or music. Some claim to be equally expert in both areas. If you are not able to find or afford a studio which specialises in voice recording you will have to choose the most suitable music studio that you can find. In choosing the right studio there are two major considerations: the engineer and the equipment. At the lower end of the financial scale there are two kinds of music studios. Those that specialise in recording classical music often have a very helpful engineer and not much equipment; those that specialise in rock music usually have huge quantities of equipment and engineers who prefer things louder, faster and heavier. You are probably better off going to the classical studio. But on the other hand . . .

Asking the following questions will help in the decision-making process.

Have you recorded speaking voices before?
The answer you are looking for is, obviously, yes! But check that they have recorded the unaccompanied voice.

What kind of mic will you use?
The best are large diaphragm condenser microphones.

What make?
Good names to listen for are Neuman, AKG, Audio-Technica, and Rode. If you hear the name Shure (sometimes pronounced Shaw) ask which model. The SM57 and SM58 are most suited to rock and pop vocals and are not good for speaking voices.

Do you have a vocal or voice booth?
If not, ask if it is possible to construct one using acoustic screens or even mattresses, cushions and carpets. If you record in a large space it will have the wrong acoustic for voice-over recording. It will be excellent for flute or drums but not right for voice.

Do you have a foldback system?
You are going to need to hear your voice and possibly music and sound effects in your headphones.

Can you do 'drop-ins'?
If they cannot you are either going to have to get everything right in a single take or pay for extra editing time when you have finished recording.

Do you have multitrack facilities?
This allows you to record a piece of music on to the main tape recorder (or computer), listen to it, and record your voice on to a

separate track without the music and voice being mixed together. On an eight-track recorder you can have two tracks of stereo music and up to six other tracks of voice, each of which can be a different take. You pick the best of the takes or make one composite by combining the best elements of all the tracks. You then add any necessary sound effects and mix the final voice, music and SFX at the right relative levels and record this mix on to a mastering machine.

What is the format of your mastering machine?
DAT is best, tape is acceptable, cassette or MiniDisc are not desirable.

Can you make CDs?
CD is the best medium for your finished recordings. If the studio does not have a CD burner (recorder) you will need your master on a DAT tape.

Do you have library (production) music?
A good tape will need more than just the bare voice. You will need to have music – preferably the kind of music which normally accompanies commercials and narrations. This is usually only available to professional studios which have a licence to store and use it.

Do you have a sound effects library?
If you are reading a narration about seagulls you will benefit from appropriate music and the sounds of the sea and seagulls.

What outboard equipment do you have?
You will probably need a compressor and maybe a de-esser as well. A good echo and reverb unit will supply the special acoustic needed for the 'haunted house' or the 'baronial hall'.

Are there any 'hidden' extras over and above the agreed hourly rate?
Watch out for VAT (sales tax), charges for DATS, CDs, cassettes, tea, coffee, water, sandwiches, and use fees for music and FX.

Three hours is the absolute minimum time required for a beginner to make enough good recordings to interest employers. In three hours you should be able to record three 30-second commercials and a two-minute narration complete with music and sound effects. This might not sound much for three hours' work but it is a realistic estimate of what it is possible for a beginner to achieve.

CONTENT OF THE TAPE

There is much disagreement over what constitutes a good tape, and you will have to decide exactly what you are going to record long before you go into the studio. There is no one tape which will cover all applications. If you make a tape which contains three commercials – soft sell, hard sell, real person spot – and one commentary, it is a well known fact that whoever listens to the tape will find that the track that interests them the least will be the very first thing they hear! Whatever interests them the most will have miraculously moved itself to the end of the tape. I have come to the conclusion that the ideal tape contains only one item – the one that gets you employed. The secret is to find out what it is that would most interest each recipient.

Most voice agents, advertising agents and casting directors will tell you that the thing that interests them most is your natural speaking voice. They are not initially interested in how many different accents or silly voices you can do. They will be more interested in hearing your normal voice in a variety of emotional situations – happy, sexy, serious, funny, etc. It is hard enough to get these right in your own voice without trying to do them as another character in a different dialect or accent. The voice business, like film and theatre, has moved towards type casting. If a creative director asks for a '35-year-old married mother of two with a university education and a soft Dublin accent' he will expect to get exactly what he has asked for. It's no good saying 'I can do that' and practising your Dublin accent. Which Dublin accent? There are 18 different ones!

Most people go into a studio and record as much material as possible in the time available. They have their recordings transferred to CD and can then make their own cassette tapes to send out. Each tape can be varied according to the needs and interests of the recipient. When you go into the studio you are not making a tape – you are recording a library of items from which different tapes can be made. It is important to record to the highest possible standard. It is no good trying to record 10 different commercials if they are not to the right standard. One minute of excellence will serve you far better than ten minutes of mediocrity.

The Copy

You must choose, and work on, material that reveals your strengths. Listen to the radio and television and pick commercials that are easily within your range. Opt for commercials that suit your sex and vocal age – on tape some people sound as much as twenty years older or younger than their actual age. Only pick one script from each category; there is no point in recording two similar chocolate scripts or two furniture warehouse 'shouters'. The easiest way to gather material is to record two or three hours of radio or television and then fast-forward through the tapes, paying attention only to the commercials. When you have chosen the ones you want, time them and write out the words. Make a note of the style and timing of any music or FX that go with them.

Commentary and narration material can be taken from TV and radio programmes. It can also be found on the Internet or be adapted from books or magazines. It is best to find something lasting about two minutes with a beginning, middle and end. Find suitable music and make a note of any sound effects that would help bring it to life. Contact your chosen studio to see if they have the music or FX you require. FX discs can be ordered from record shops and individual SFX can be downloaded from the Internet at a reasonable price.

Your scripts should be typed, double or triple spaced, and should not be in capitals. We rely on capital letters to alert us to proper nouns and new sentences. A script entirely in capital letters is very hard to read and even harder to make sense of. Use a fresh sheet of paper for each script and do not type on both sides of the paper. The scripts should have a note of their duration and the entry and exit points for music and SFX should be clearly marked. You will need three copies of each script – one for you, one for the engineer, and one for your producer.

THE PRODUCER

If you go into a studio without a producer you risk wasting both your time and money. If you are using a music studio the engineer will have little or no experience of voice recording and will be no help to you beyond telling you that you got a word wrong or that you read the script in 32 seconds instead of 29. There are very few producers who can combine the job of engineering, directing and producing, all to the same high standard. You are entering a market in which there is fierce competition – even for the lower paid jobs. Your recordings have to be to the highest possible standard; there can be no excuses or mitigating circumstances. You have to get it right.

You need someone to act as your producer. They may not be an audio producer but they do have to be someone who you can trust to tell you the truth as they hear it. Your parents or your partner will tell you that you are wonderful. That is not what you want to hear in the studio. You need someone who has worked through the material with you, who knows what you are trying to achieve with each script and who will tell you, honestly, how you are doing. Make sure that you have agreed on phrasing and inflection. Pay special attention to your narration script. You have probably chosen something with a strong visual element like a wildlife script or a travelogue. The recordings you will be doing in the studio are for audio use only. There will be no pictures to support them so you and your producer should work hard at getting your delivery to generate pictures in the mind of the listener. Choose appropriate music and sound effects to help you.

When you are in the studio you can ask for a playback of each take, but this wastes time and time costs money. Your producer should be able to tell you, through talkback, if it was a bad take, what was wrong with it and therefore save you from having to waste time listening to it.

The most common problems for your producer to listen out for are:

- sloppy diction
- sounding as if you are reading
- slight hesitation on a word
- not 'lifting' the product
- incorrect pitch patterns
- making a phone number instantly forgettable
- breathing in the wrong places
- breathing too noisily
- sounding panicked as you come towards the end of a script
- going down in the wrong places
- not smiling – sounding miserable
- not creating pictures on a narration script
- making a question into a statement
- changing the script (the ultimate sin)
- overprojection – popping
- shouting
- inconsistent volume
- sounding condescending
- sibilance
- noisy mouth or lips
- rumbling tummy
- noisy clothes or jewellery
- script rustles.

If he or she hears any of these things you should be stopped and told to start again. You might be told that the first sentence was fine but that you need to drop-in (pick up) from the second sentence. Only when your producer thinks you have a complete take should you go into the control room and listen to it on the monitors.

Running in and out of the control room every time you have recorded something is a waste of valuable time. The very best working environment is where producer, engineer and artist are all in the same space – like a modern radio studio. This can save a lot of time.

PREPARATION

If you are going to be working on a multitrack system you might end up with two good takes of one particular script. Rather than try to choose between them at the time, remember to ask for both of them to be put on to your master. You can make your decision when the studio clock is not running.

Voice recording is very tiring. All the focus of attention and pressure is going to be on you so make sure you sleep well beforehand. Don't forget to take still mineral water, biscuits, throat pastilles and tissues with you to the studio. You will also need pencils, rubbers and plain paper. Plan to get there at least 15 minutes early.

THE SESSION

When you get into the studio ask for the microphone to be adjusted so that you can stand up. Make sure there is a music stand on which to put your scripts (holding them can cause unwanted rustling sounds) and that there is enough light for you to read them easily. Get the levels in the headphones adjusted to your liking. If the music is loud you will start shouting to make yourself heard. If the music is too quiet or your voice is too loud you may not deliver the script with enough energy. It is important to get the headphone levels right and you may want them changed for each script. The 'slow and sexy' requires a different headphone balance from the 'hard and shouty'.

If you are recording a commercial that has music it is very important to hear this in the foldback in your cans. It helps you to capture the mood. If the commercial is designed so that your first word coincides exactly with the first beat of the music you will need a way of achieving this. The easiest way is to get the engineer to record the music on to his multitrack or computer and to set the clock to read zero at the start of the music. He can then count you down backwards to the start point. You will hear '5 4 3 2 1' and you start on zero. The music should be with you. He can record his count so that he does not have to do it every time you start again.

THE MASTER RECORDING

After the session you will leave with your recordings on CD or DAT. If they are on DAT you should get them transferred to CD. This will allow you to play them and decide which takes you prefer if there are choices to be made. In the USA, voice artists and their agents like to make a short collage consisting of extracts (clips) from complete commercials with no gaps between each one. The listener gets a rapid tour of the material, which is usually no longer than 90 seconds. In the UK, employers prefer to hear complete commercials although there is now a move towards making these short collage tapes. This can often be done on a PC without having to go back to a studio. It is another good reason for having your recordings on CD as most PCs can load audio direct from the CD drive. Many musicians have the software necessary to do this editing and will probably be able to make you a new CD with the collage version of your work. If you do not know anyone who can do this for you a local music shop might be able to put you in touch with someone who can help. If all else fails you may have to go back to a studio to get this done. It is unwise to attempt to make this collage at the end of the main session as you will probably be too tired to make good artistic judgements. You need to live with your recorded material for a few days before really knowing which tracks, which versions, and which order works best.

MAKING TAPES

You now have the commercials and narration recorded as separate, complete tracks, and you have the short collage version which contains extracts of all of them. The temptation is to send them off to a duplicating facility, have 500 copies made complete with expensive inlay cards and labels, and then post them out to all and sundry in the hope of receiving work. As you will see in the next chapter this approach has about the same statistical chance of success as buying a lottery ticket and expecting to become a million-aire overnight. It might work but the overwhelming evidence is that it does not!

Because one tape will not serve all applications it is necessary to make each tape individually. If you have recorded three commercials there are 15 different ways of combining them in ones, twos and threes. If you have recorded 10 commercials there are over three million ways of combining them! One need not explore all the possible combinations as it is normal to go for contrasts between adjoining tracks, and if you have two similar reads it is advisable to save one of them for use on a follow-up tape.

It is possible to make better quality cassette copies using domestic hi-fi equipment than you would get from a commercial duplicator. Most commercial duplicators make copies at high speed and, although it is quick, there is a loss of quality. Some high speed duplicating machines will only copy from a cassette so there is yet another loss of quality. Duplicators who work in what is called 'real time' take at least 30 minutes to make a copy of a 30-minute programme and are consequently quite expensive. Both systems ask you to send a DAT master with everything in the required order. If you want the order changed you will be charged for the work involved.

By connecting the output of a domestic CD player directly to the input of a domestic cassette machine you can make very high quality cassettes. The internal electronics of the average hi-fi system are not always of the highest possible quality and this method of connecting the CD to the cassette by-passes them completely. If you are not happy about doing this then route the CD to the cassette using the controls on the system. Most CD players can be pre-programmed to replay the tracks in any sequence, so once you have done this the cassette will have the tracks in your preferred order. However, there is a delay of a few seconds as the CD player changes from one track to another. To overcome this you can press the pause button on the cassette as one track finishes and release it as soon as the number of the next track is displayed on the CD player. Your voice CD should have been made with a half- to one-second delay between the track ident and the start of the recording, which is enough time for the cassette to start recording again once you release the pause button.

CASSETTES

The cassettes that you use should be the professional ones available from studio supply companies. If you buy normal cassettes from a hi-fi shop it is very unlikely that anyone will bother to listen to them. They will label you as an amateur who is not taking themselves or the business seriously. Cassettes from a hi-fi shop usually last for 45 minutes a side. Psychologically, this is a very bad thing to send someone. They are likely to look at it and decide that you are yet another amateur sending them the whole of *War and Peace*, the full version of *The Rime Of The Ancient Mariner*, and 15 pages from the Harley Davidson technical manual. They will throw it in the bin without listening to it. Most tapes – especially unsolicited ones – are not listened to!

Cassettes from a hi-fi shop have a labelling system which allows for only three or four words in small writing. You need to have your name and phone number writ large on the body of the cassette. Shop cassettes use the cassette to advertise the cassette itself – how long it is, which tape it is, and which company manufactured it. The inlay card (also referred to as a J card) carries all the same information and has very little space for the important things like your name and telephone number. Do not use non-professional cassettes.

The best looking professional cassettes come in a plain black shell which has space for the full-size cassette label. It is possible to buy these cassettes in other colours – red, gold, green, blue and white are the most popular ones. They can be bought with transparent shells, although these look rather strange once the label is put on them. Colours other than black look cheap and are usually associated with children's songs and stories.

The cassettes can be bought loaded with either chrome or ferric tape. Chrome is best for music reproduction and the slightly cheaper ferric is better for speech programmes. Speech recorded on chrome tape can suffer from increased sibilance and the listener may well assume that you sound like that naturally! These tapes can be bought for any length of programme, although there may be an extra charge for unusual lengths. The standard lengths are 5, 10, 20 and 30 minutes. Longer lengths are available but they are not necessary for voice tapes. These are the total running times for the cassette, so the five-minute tape will be two and a half minutes per side – the right length for commercials. The C10 is perfect for narration and the C20 ideal for radio drama and drama tapes. Nobody is going to listen for more than 10 minutes and most will not go beyond two! Do not send out double-sided tapes – the only thing that should be on the 'B' side is a straight repeat of the 'A' side. If you buy professional tapes from a reputable studio supply company, the price for 10 is the same as the price for 50. It is only when you buy more than a hundred that there is a reduction in price.

Art Work

The company that sells you the cassettes will probably be able to sell you the blank cassette labels as well. These either come on tractor feed rolls of 500 or on A4 sheets of 12 or 16 to a sheet. The labels on rolls work very well with word processors if you put them in the centre of the roller and set the machine to 'centre' the text. After a little experimentation it is easy to work out the line spacing that will print above and below the central cut-out.

Labels on A4 sheets can be used on computers that have label printing software – Microsoft Windows for example. There are several very good software packages that you can buy which not only allow you to print labels but also give you design templates and clip-art packages to further improve your packaging. These are often designed to work only with their own label packages but they do produce astonishingly professional results. The cassette label should be printed with your name and telephone numbers. It must say, in one word, what is on the cassette – commercials, narrations, industrials, drama, radio drama, children's stories, etc. There should be an identical label on both sides of the cassette.

Your cassette should also have an inlay card (J card) to go inside the box. Blank versions of these can be obtained from the tape supplier but, because they are so small, it is very difficult to print on them. It is possible to use pre-printed sticky labels, but again, this is the mark of the amateur. Inlay cards do not have to be made from card – they can be made from thick paper and cut and folded to fit. They should have the same information as is on the label as well as a photograph of you.

If your voice and your 'image' do not match, the photograph could do more harm than good as you might be incorrectly stereotyped. Some lady voice-overs of a certain age specialise in playing sexy voiced twenty-somethings. It might not be to their advantage to put a photograph on the inlay card. If your voice and your image match, however, you could double your chances of employment! Creative directors cast 'people' as well as 'voices' and most of them look at the box while listening to the cassette. You could be invited to be 'in' the commercial!

It is possible to print two inlay cards on to a sheet of A4 paper. The photograph can be scanned into a home computer and placed on to each of the inlay cards. Guidelines can be printed so that the cards can be accurately cut (using scissors or guillotine) to fit the cassette box. Neato, who make the cassette labelling software, include J card printing software with it. However, you do have to use their blank cards.

The total cost of sending out a professional cassette with a printed label and inlay card should work out to be less than buying a cassette from a hi-fi store.

COMPACT DISCS

It is becoming increasingly fashionable, especially in the USA, for individual voice artists to send their work out on CD rather than cassette. It used to be only voice agents who sent out a CD compilation of all their artists. The price of CDs has dropped and it is now possible to manufacture a CD and print a label and Jewel Case insert on a home computer for about £1.40 ($2). Most voice agents and advertising agents in the UK are still equipped to deal with voice cassettes, however. They have specially manufactured shelving systems to accommodate them and there is the risk that a CD which does not fit on the shelf with the other voice tapes might get overlooked!

Whether you send out CD or cassette, make sure that it is recorded and manufactured to the highest possible standard. The voice world is a highly competitive business and in order to succeed you have to pay the greatest possible attention to even the smallest of details.

Don't refer to, or think of, your recordings as a 'demo'. A 'demo' is what you might possibly be able to do on a good day if only somebody would give you a chance. What you send out is a voice tape or a voice CD – nothing less.

9

Finding Work

VOICE AGENTS

Having made their tape most aspiring voice artists assume that the next step is to find a voice agent. Voice agents will be eager to sign them up because they are talented, and versatile, and all the happy voice artist has to do is sit back, wait for the phone to ring, and decide what to do with the large sums of money that will undoubtedly come their way. With that attitude you might as well spend all your money on a lottery ticket!

You have to ask yourself the question: Why would a voice agent be interested in me? Being 'good' or even 'talented' is not enough. Being 'versatile' is of little interest to anyone! In which advertising agency meeting does the creative director say, 'What we need is a versatile voice'? They don't. They ask for something specific, defined by age, sex, accent and attitude. The only occasions you are likely to hear a request for 'versatile' are casting sessions for talking books, children's story reading, and animations.

Voice agents work on 10 per cent commission in the USA, and as much as 15 per cent commission plus 17.5 per cent VAT (sales tax) in the UK. They have a vested interest in representing and selling 'expensive' voices. They are keen to represent anyone with a high public profile who would be prepared to lend their name, their voice, and even their face to a sales campaign. In the UK, a very well-known police chief started endorsing home security products within weeks of his retirement. A few months later he was extolling the safety features of a particular brand of tyre. For many years a British World Heavyweight boxing champion was the voice, the face, and the armpit of a well-known range of men's toiletries. A French football player endorses the Eurostar Trains which run between London and Paris. These people have not had any acting experience, they did not make voice tapes, and whether they are 'good' or not is very much open to debate. However, none of them would have any difficulty in finding a voice agent to represent them.

If you send your new voice tape, beautifully packaged, complete with covering letter, CV and photograph to any one of the London voice agents they will probably put it in a cardboard box with all the others they received in the last four weeks. In another four weeks time they are quite likely to empty the box into the dustbin to make room for the next batch of unsolicited tapes. A better approach is to call them on the telephone – it saves both time and money. You can ask if they are listening to tapes and, if so, what would interest them at the moment. Unfortunately, it may be a painful experience! Your call is quite likely to be answered by a 22-year-old girl who has been in the voice business for all of two and a half months and already knows all there is to know about it. She will probably tell you to go away – except that those might not be the words she uses. If she's feeling in a good mood she may confine herself to telling you that their books are full and they will not be listening to any tapes in the next six months.

If you did manage to acquire a voice agent what would happen to you? You would probably be right down at the bottom of the heap. It is a well-known fact that the sole purpose of the bottom of any heap is to provide a resting place for the illustrious souls at the top. In the event that your new agency is asked to recommend a voice for a commercial they will immediately start with the 'famous' names charging the largest fees, then work their way slowly down the financial ladder until they sell someone. They are unlikely to get to you and neither will they ever make you their first recommendation. I know a voice artist who has been working nearly every day for the last three years, and yet the famous agency to which she is signed have yet to get her a job. She is convinced that they don't even know who she is!

There are some good voice agents who will treat you sympathetically and they seem to be the ones who have a presence on the Internet. A couple have very interesting Websites complete with pages of information for newcomers. Their details can be found in chapter 14.

REGIONAL ACCENTS

There is one set of circumstances in which a voice agent may well be interested in you. Most of them pride themselves on maintaining a least one 'voice' in all of the popular categories. They divide their categories into male and female, then into age groups, character, national accents, regional accents, and local accents. So they would pride themselves on being able to supply voices as diverse as a 'Comedy French/Canadian Gangster' or a 'Transvestite Liverpudlian Taxidriver'. If their resident Scottish voice (soft highland accent) has gone to the great distillery in the sky they will be looking for a replacement. If you phone them and, by coincidence, you have a genuine Highland accent, they might well be interested in you. They will want to be reassured that your accent is genuine as no advertiser would knowingly use a fake. A fake accent would detract from the credibility of the commercial and all genuine Highlanders would be aware of the deception. It is only in humorous and satirical commercials that a fake accent might be considered acceptable and there would be no attempt made to disguise the forgery.

IMPERSONATIONS

Another popular misconception is that voice agents will be very keen to sign up anyone who can do impersonations. If an advertiser wants a famous voice they will book them. Using someone to do an impersonation sounds 'cheap' and is fraught with legal difficulties. Using an impersonation to promote a product is not the same as including one in a comedy or light entertainment show. There have been cases where a celebrity has successfully sued an advertiser for damages when their 'voice' has been used without either permission or payment. If you copied a famous cola bottle and sold your own cola in it you would expect to be sued for infringement of copyright. A 'voice' is the intellectual property of the person using or owning it – while they are alive.

ADVERTISING AGENCIES

Having established the fact that voice agents are unlikely to be interested in you, the question is who will? The answer is advertising agencies and commercial radio stations.

In the mid-1990s in the UK there was an industrial dispute between the voice artists and the advertising agencies during which time the voice artists withdrew their labour. The advertising agencies had to continue making commercials and they discovered that they could use non-union 'amateurs' for voice-overs. Some of these people were good and some were not, but, given modern technology and a degree of patience, it was always possible to get or 'make' a satisfactory performance. As a result, nearly all big advertising agencies now have voice departments or, at the very least, someone who is responsible for listening to and cataloguing voice tapes. In the USA there is a long tradition of non-union talent without a voice agent getting work directly from advertising agencies. They may get a lower level of pay and they may not get residual (repeat) payments, but they use this work to build a career and eventually achieve both union membership and an agent. Unions on both sides of the Atlantic operate a psychological 'Catch 22' situation – you can't do the job unless you are in the union but you can't join the union unless you do the job. The UK union for voice artists is Equity; in the USA it is either SAG or AFTRA.

If the bad news is that voice agents are unlikely to be interested in you, then the good news is that you don't need one and you don't need to be in a union. The very good news is that you can get work directly from the advertising agencies and radio stations.

The easy way to find advertising agencies is by looking in Yellow Pages. There are several other publications which list the agencies, and one in the UK which gives the contact name of the person dealing with voices – although these can change at short notice!

The temptation is to start by contacting the biggest and the best agencies. It might be a better policy to approach the smaller 'out of town' ones. They are likely to be handling low budget radio and television commercials and either unwilling or unable to pay the high fees expected by union members. Smaller agencies may be less experienced in dealing with voice artists and this gives you the chance to learn how to conduct yourself without making mistakes that will blight your future career.

FINDING WORK

The best way to approach all agencies is by telephone. Write yourself a script along the lines of: 'Hello, my name is Arthur Crundale and I'm a voice-over artist. I'm going to send you a copy of my voice tape but I have a lot of material and I don't want to waste your time so perhaps you'd like to tell me what would interest you at the moment? Are you about to cast anything?' A script like this puts you at a distinct psychological advantage. It is a mistake to ask someone if you can send them a tape – it gives them the chance to say no! *Tell* them you are going to send the tape; their input into the situation is that you give them the chance to choose what goes on it. Car salesman never ask a prospect if she is going to 'buy' the car. They always follow a stream of positives: 'Will you have it in red or green, will you have two door or four door, will you have cassette or CD; will you pay cash or instalments?' The same technique works when selling the voice. You have to use the voice to sell the voice and if you cannot sell your own voice how can you sell a product? Advertising agencies will warm to you if you demonstrate an understanding of the psychology of selling. You are offering yourself as a potential solution to the 'problem' they may have of finding someone to voice their next commercial.

It is a good idea to buy (or at least read) the advertising trade papers. They always carry news of who has won a recent contract, who the new creative directors are, and which group of strangely named people have decided to set up yet another agency. This insider information can be invaluable when talking to agency personnel as it makes you sound informed about their business. I have known voice artists to contact creative directors with suggestions for a new angle on a campaign which, of course, involves one of their own unique voices. It can get results!

When you phone the agency have what you want to say prepared in the form of a script. Stand up to make the call – you sound more confident and authoritative when you stand. Your phone call is rather like an audition – they will be evaluating your voice as you talk to them, and having a script prevents you from getting tongue tied or losing your train of thought. Your script may only be 58 words but some national TV commercials are only 10 words and you would certainly have a script for them!

If they are not casting anything at the time you call they will probably ask you to send an example of your ordinary speaking voice – no funny voices, no accents. Agencies are always most interested in your natural voice. Do what they ask and send them one example of your natural voice reading a commercial script, with or without music and FX. Resist the temptation to send them your Sean Connery or Barbra Streisand impression. Anything other than what they have asked for will only serve to confuse them. They do not want 'versatile'. The advertising voice world works on type casting and they are definitely not interested in your classical acting abilities.

Remember – the ideal tape contains only one item, the one that gets you employed. Your tape is the key to the door and you want to get your foot in the door of the voice-over world. The time to display your versatility and other talents is when you are an established and trusted performer.

The chain of command and decision-making is longer and more complicated in advertising agencies than it is in commercial radio stations. In radio you usually only work with the commercial producer. There may be an engineer but most commercial producers can drive a desk. In ad agencies you could be faced with six or seven people. There is a largely true saying that 'you do seven takes for every person in the control room'.

A joke popular in voice circles seeks to know the difference between a toilet and voice artist. The answer being that the toilet only has to stare at one posterior at a time. There is another side to the story, however – the people in the control room can have problems dealing with the voice artist. At the end of a difficult ad agency session involving many retakes and much cutting and splicing of words, a creative director was heard to turn to the voice artist and say, 'There, that's perfect. Don't you wish you could do it like that?' Working for an ad agency can sometimes be hard and frustrating work and this is reflected in the much higher rates of pay.

RADIO STATIONS

Commercial radio stations, especially those 'out of town', will be pleased to hear from you as they are always in need of new voices. There is a limit to the number of times they can use local voices without the advertisers and the listeners noticing.

Commercial radio stations receive no public subsidy and no licence fee income. They generate their income by selling on-air advertising time and, having done that, they sell their production skills in creating commercials for the advertisers. The selling of the on-air time is under the control of the sales manager and the commercials are made by the commercial producer and his team. The commercial producer deals with voice artists. He may also be a voice artist and so he can voice some of the commercials himself. He is usually a he!

Some voice-over artists choose to work as touring actors and they are very happy to accept parts in shows which travel up and down the country. When they know which towns and cities they are going to visit they alert local radio stations and advertising agencies to their impending visit and offer their services as an 'out of town' voice. This can be quite lucrative and it gives both the creative and commercial directors a chance to offer their clients a 'special' voice for which they might well charge a premium. This may (or may not!) be passed on to the actor. Other actors pretend that they are going to be in a certain locality on a specified day as an equally successful way of creating work!

PAY SCALES

The rate of pay for voicing a single local radio commercial is so low (£8, £10 or £14 in the UK) that it is hardly worth travelling to a radio station to do it. These commercials are paid for on a per script basis and not according to the time it takes to do them. Commercial producers want you in and out of the studio as quickly as possible, so if you take more than 15 minutes per script you will probably not get another booking.

Advertising agencies have a very different way of paying voice-over artists. The union rates in the UK in the year 2000 are approximately £125 per hour for recording the commercial (radio or television) plus a further fee payable when it is transmitted (a 'use fee') of anything from a few pounds for radio to several thousand pounds for national television. Famous voices do not work for these fees (or anything like them) and will probably negotiate 'residuals', which are fees paid every time the commercial is transmitted. Advertising agencies are trying to phase out residuals in the UK so they are unlikely to be offered to newcomers and people who are not members of unions. The dispute in the mid-1990s was caused by the attempted removal of residual payments.

Because of the huge difference between the two pay scales local radio stations try to offer a 'package' deal to make visiting them more worthwhile. The commercial producer will assemble a number of scripts for one person to work on during the one session. He may be looking for a degree of versatility and even a few funny voices. For example:

- a nerdy voice as part of a computer commercial
- a straight read for a charity appeal
- a romantic voice for the flower shop
- henpecked husband as half of a male/female argument for fitted kitchens (the female voice will do her part on another day)
- a hard sell for the local furniture warehouse
- an on-air promo for one of the stations forthcoming 'specials'.

An actor who can 'talk to himself' might find it easier to get work on this circuit, especially if he can play a range of zany characters within the same commercial and do the smooth 'announcer tag' at the end of it.

The voice artist will be expected to make each of these voices sound 'different' so that the casual listener will not realise that two consecutive ads were voiced by the same person. It is unlikely that one person would be asked to voice commercials for businesses that are in competition or conflict with each other. You would not be asked to do two garage commercials, and neither would you be asked to advertise a funeral parlour and a Chinese restaurant.

Commercial radio stations have a vested interest in paying you as little as possible. Commercial production provides a large part of their profits and the commercial producer often relies on a percentage of those profits to help feed his family. He agrees a production budget with an advertiser and then attempts to spend as little of it as possible. It is quite possible for him to charge £1000 ($1,600) to produce a spot and then spend only £30 ($50) making it. Advertising agencies agree a budget with their client and then make a point of spending every last penny of it. They will spend even more if they think they can get away with it. They make their profit by surcharging the client 17 per cent on top of everything they spend on their behalf. If they happen to have their own 'in house' scriptwriter, director, engineer and studio they will charge for these at the going rate and then charge an additional 17 per cent on top. In theory, radio stations pay you as little as possible; ad agencies pay you as much as possible.

The terms and conditions of job offers are usually pre-determined. You are likely to get a call which will say, 'Are you free to do a commercial on Friday at 3pm in City Studios. The fee is £750 ($1,200)?' Everything has been decided in advance and is non-negotiable. All you can say is 'Yes' or 'No'. If you are not available they will move on very quickly to the next person on their list. If you do not feel prepared to work for a £750 fee, say so. They will probably move on without offering you more. The worst thing you can do is call them back saying 'I've changed my mind about the fee. I am prepared to . . .'. If you do this you will lose all credibility. Either you work for £750 or you don't.

When the fee is negotiable the question will be 'How much would you charge for a session on Friday at 3pm in City Studios'? The best course of action is to find out as much as possible about the job before committing yourself. Who is the final client? What is the product? A multinational corporation would expect to pay a lot more for a voice than the flower shop in the high street. Remember, in the big boys' world, expensive is better! Charge accordingly.

ISDN

The relatively low fees and rapid advances in digital technology have revolutionised the way local radio commercials are made. Most voices and producers on this circuit rely on ISDN – the International Standard Digital Network – which is used to send high quality digital information around the world. The main piece of electronic equipment required is a Codec (Coder/Decoder) which converts the sound from a microphone into digital information. A high quality microphone, headphones, and a fax machine are also required. The telephone company has to install an ISDN line which is higher quality than normal domestic lines. This is a lot more expensive in the UK than in the USA, although prices have started to fall.

The microphone and headphones are plugged in to the Codec and it is plugged into the ISDN telephone line. Contact can now be made with similar equipment anywhere in the world. A radio station wanting to use a voice artist over the ISDN line would first telephone them on the ordinary telephone line to check availability and fees. A script is faxed through and the voice artist switches the Codec on at the required time. The commercial producer phones the voice artist on the ISDN number and they can now talk to each other with studio quality sound. The voice artist can hear any music or FX used in the production in the headphones, as well as the directions from the producer. If the script is a 'two hander' there may be a second voice artist 'patched in' from yet another part of the country. The only problem with ISDN is that very few voice people can afford to have a soundproofed booth or room built in which to house it. There is always the problem of the microphone picking up unwanted noises. Traffic is the worst of these, but others include children, pets, televisions, vacuum cleaners, hi-fi systems, neighbours, aeroplanes and trains. Some people build themselves a soundproofed booth in the cupboard under the stairs or in the basement or garage. Others rely on co-operation from the family! A few talking books are now done on ISDN – five days is a long time to expect family co-operation! Some people have gone someway to overcoming this problem by getting voice jobs for their children so that they too feel part of the enterprise.

Certain radio stations are centralising their commercial production facilities in areas where property and living costs are cheaper than in the big cities. The voice artist who actually goes into their local station may still be working over ISDN lines. Some advertising agencies and voice agents have also invested in the equipment. In the USA, advertising agencies are inviting voice artists to submit auditions for a particular script over ISDN lines. Some of these operate like telephone answering machines so an ad agency can collect auditions over a 24-hour period and then replay them all at the same time.

ISDN is making it possible for the voice artist to work anywhere in the world from the comfort of their own home.

NARRATION WORK

Narration is 'telling' rather than 'selling'. Artistically, it can be very satisfying, and narrating wildlife documentaries is seen as being the very pinnacle of success in the voice business. Narration does not necessarily pay as much as commercial voice-overs, but some jobs, if they are sold and repeated all over the world, can be more productive than a pension fund – it depends on your contract.

In its simplest form narration can involve providing the commentary for a film made by a community group or local charity. Many people can point a video camera in roughly the right direction, and there are low-cost facility houses which can edit amateur videos into something suitable for public exhibition. But they nearly always need a professional voice – and probably a professional scriptwriter as well. Every man and his dog seems to be in the video business and Yellow Pages has an impossibly large number of entries under the relevant classifications. Contacting these companies can be a very good way to get a foot on the commentary ladder. They are unlikely to know where to find professional voice-over artists so most of them will be grateful to be contacted. You can be the solution to a problem they might not have realised they had.

These people should be contacted by telephone with the suggestion that you could call in and introduce yourself, and at the same time give them a voice tape. One of the problems associated with working for one man (and his dog) companies is getting paid. They will be reluctant to part with anything like a professional fee, but it should be made clear that whatever you agree on as fair remuneration should be paid on the day of recording – preferably in cash! Working for these video companies will acquaint you with the most dreadful scripts and primitive sound recording equipment. These are the people who see a toilet (washroom) as the ideal voice booth.

VIDEO COMPANIES

Further up the scale there are more established companies making good quality professional videos and films for small businesses. These will also appear in Yellow Pages and will be members of a professional association or, at the very least, the local chamber of trade or commerce. These companies can be a very good source of both income and experience. They are likely to be making product information films, training films, tourist board videos, educational programmes, and some of them will be making a few low budget television commercials. They will all need professional voices.

When companies of this size start editing their material they often have a guide voice track which they put on the first rough (off line) edit. The final version may well have a minor celebrity or local TV personality reading the script. A good way of getting your foot in the door of the smaller video and film companies is to offer to do a guide voice for little or no pay. Make it clear that you will only do this once as an introductory offer – it is too easy to get categorised as someone who is prepared to work for little or no pay. Once you have got this label it is almost impossible to shake off. Remember – the labourer is worthy of his hire!

LOCAL TV COMMERCIALS

Companies in this range who are producing TV commercials may well find it difficult to get suitable voice artists. They are unable to use the local TV personalities as their terms of employment will prevent them from endorsing commercial products both in and out of vision. Consequently, when your foot is firmly in their door, give them a copy of your commercials tape. Local TV commercials are not very exciting – a few still photos which are manipulated by a digital effects generator, off the shelf library music, and a voice-over saying:

> *Dreamline's summer sale of fine bedding and furniture has just started at 47 The High Street Small-town. There's 20 per cent off everything and there's 12 months interest-free credit (written details on request). Remember – Dreamline, 47 The High Street, Small-town – for finer furniture and better bedding. Dreamline.*

There is quite an art in making a script as boring and banal as this sound interesting.

BROADCAST WORK

At the top of the scale are the film and video companies who work mainly in the broadcast field. This includes all the television channels – terrestrial, satellite, digital and cable. Some TV stations originate very few programmes themselves but rely on buying in or commissioning work from specialist programme makers. One way of finding out who does what is to watch as much of the relevant output as possible. However, there are far too many TV stations for one person to monitor them all. Some listings magazines give production credits, telling you the names of the director, producer, production company, and voice-over. Another trick is to video much of the output of a particular station and to watch only the closing credits of each programme. You will soon be able to build up a picture of who is doing what and for whom.

There is also a lot of information available on the Internet. The BBC, for example, has one of the best and busiest websites in the world where you can find many production details and very often complete scripts and transcripts.

Many specialist publications list broadcast production companies and give details of their most recent productions. Having seen a company credited on screen the only way to find out more about them can be to consult these trade books. Unfortunately, they can be very expensive – as much as £100 ($160) each – but reference libraries should have access to them.

In the UK there is an on-line service called Production News which lists broadcast programmes in their various stages of completion. They have sections for 'In Development', 'In Pre-Production', 'In Production', 'In Post-Production', and (hopefully) 'Completed'. They give details of the nature of the project, the producer, the director, and a contact number for the production company concerned. This is a wonderful source of information and it is usually months ahead of the usual tip sheets and casting information services. This information can be received as a monthly publication, but both this and the on-line service are very expensive. However, it only takes one job to pay for it many times over!

When approaching major broadcast production companies it is important to be realistic in what you suggest yourself for. You only get one chance to make a first impression and the usual actor's response of 'I can do that' might not see you taken seriously. If you are contacting a company making natural history films for world-wide release narrated by famous actors, it is pointless to suggest that you could narrate some of them, unless, of course, you are also a famous actor. If you are a famous actor it is unlikely that you would be phoning them in the first place. What you could suggest is that you do some of the guide voices or work on a less high profile project. The important thing is to get a foot in the door and to be treated as a serious professional.

Some companies ask their regular recording studio to suggest voices for particular projects. It is a good idea to identify the studios most often used for voice recording and give them a copy of your tape. Most voice-orientated studios maintain a library of voice tapes and are happy to recommend voices to clients. Recording engineers have a very realistic picture of how quick and easy it is to work with particular voice artists.

NON-COMMERCIAL RADIO STATIONS

Many speech-based radio stations employ voices for narration work. They can be used to read letters, statements, translations, reports, book extracts, etc. The list is endless. Sometimes they find the readers among their existing non-broadcasting staff – particularly when they want an 'amateur' feel. The PM programme on BBC Radio 4 often uses their own office staff as the on-air readers of listeners' letters. Documentaries and consumer programmes usually use professional voice artists. For work in news-based programmes approach the editor; for documentary and consumer programmes approach the relevant director.

TELEPHONE WORK

There are many jobs that can be done from the comfort of the voice artist's own home using the ordinary telephone network without having to invest in ISDN lines and equipment. The telephone information industry is growing rapidly, fuelled by the profits to be made by encouraging people to call premium rate numbers.

These lines charge a lot more than ordinary ones and a percentage of the cost goes to the person or company being called. One very popular business is in offering multiple choice information lines where, for example, the caller can hear a series of pre-recorded messages describing the merits (or otherwise) of various makes of car. Other popular subjects are health matters, gardening problems, film reviews, sports reports, racing results, and so on.

Many banks now offer a telephone banking service where the caller is asked to follow a series of voice prompts. Even the telephone service providers seem to have dispensed with people in favour of recorded messages – real people are only used as a very last resort.

A lot of the companies engaged in these activities employ voice artists to record the announcements and information from their own telephones. The script is sent a few days in advance of the proposed recording date, together with the telephone number of the producer. The voice artist can call the producer to discuss any pronunciations or inflections that might need clarifying. When the voice artist is ready to record they call the company computer on a special number and commence work. The buttons on the telephone become the recording controls so that pressing 1 starts the recording, 2 stops it, 3 replays it, and 4 erases it. When a satisfactory recording is made, the number 78 is pressed and the receiving computer stores it in its memory. It is rather like recording a new message on a remote-controlled telephone answering machine. Payment for these jobs is in two parts: a fee for studying and preparing the scripts and an hourly rate for recording them. The employer's computer is able to tell how long you were 'logged on'.

CD ROMS AND COMPUTER GAMES

This is one of the biggest growth areas in voice work. An astonishingly high proportion of homes now have at least one computer and, despite all protestations to the contrary, most of them are used for nothing more useful than playing games. There is fierce competition between the games manufacturers and they are getting more and more new games out on to the market as quickly as possible. Nearly all of these use voices and, as with radio commercials, this is where versatility is prized.

The designers of these games have to be very cost-conscious so they use as few voice artists as possible to play the many characters in the game. Most of the characters in a game do not speak to each other – they only address the player – so the scripts are recorded as a series of statements rather than conversations. This means that all the speeches for one character can be recorded together before moving on to the speeches for an entirely different character. Two or three versatile voice artists can populate a game with hundreds of different characters, with some of the voices being altered by electronic processing.

To get this kind of work you need to send a tape which demonstrates your versatility within this fantasy medium. You should write your own five-minute script containing as many believable voices as you can manage. Make good use of music and effects and make it sound like the soundtrack of a busy game or cartoon. These kinds of tapes take at least a whole day to record and mix, but the time (and money) is well spent because the same tape can also be sent to animation studios for work in cartoons.

The market for educational and instructional software is growing almost as fast as the games market. One of the most sought after features in any computer is the very latest sound and graphics system. All new home computers are sold with a software bundle and the size and value of these do as much to sell the computer as anything else. Most publishers of school books are transferring them to interactive CD Roms with, at the very least, voice prompts. Language courses are also moving away from cassette and CD formats and their programmes are now available on CD Rom.

There is a vast amount of work available in the educational field. It is worth spending time in a computer shop writing down the names and addresses of the publishers of this kind of software and contacting them direct. They are interested in friendly, well-modulated voices, and the UK language teaching companies are very keen to have regional accents. They are trying to get away from the 'Oxford English' approach. Some of the publishers of this material offer voice test auditions in their own studios. They will give you a range of material to record which they then store in their archives and refer to when casting new projects. These auditions are by appointment only.

INTERNET

The Internet is revolutionising the voice world. Putting the words 'voice-over' into a search engine produces a mass of websites. All voice agents will have to have a website in the very near future. The good ones already do and they have the facility to play their clients showreels over the Internet while displaying a picture and a biography. Their sites can be searched by sex, age, accent and voice type so that you only need listen to the ones that really interest you.

Many voice artists have their own individual sites which give pages of information and play extracts from their various voice tapes. There are bulletin boards where notices and questions are posted and where people can advertise themselves in a less expensive way than maintaining their own website.

Showbusiness publications such as *The Stage* are also available on-line and can be checked every Thursday morning for voice-over job advertisements.

COMMUNICATION

Many voice jobs are offered at very short notice so it is important that you can be contacted quickly, easily and reliably. At the very least you should have an ordinary phone with a remote access answering machine. Having a mobile phone with a messaging service is even better. They are rapidly replacing ordinary phones as you can carry them with you at all times.

One very busy voice artist, famed for the way he said 'probably', had a good way of making sure he was always available for work. Every morning his 'man' would drive him to the heart of the Soho studio district in London and they would either cruise round or park and read the paper. The mobile phone was switched on and they sat and waited. The advertising world knew that he was there and available for work. He made a lot of money by always being in the right place at the right time.

ON THE JOB

No effort is wasted, and providing you have put enough care and energy into the pursuit of work you are likely to find it sooner or later. If finding work is hard then doing it is even harder! Here are some points to pay particular attention to when the big day comes!

(1) Avoid dairy products, tea and coffee the day before. Drink little or no alcohol. Get an early night.

(2) Dress in quiet clothing – neither too smart nor too casual. Do not use perfume or aftershave. Wear comfortable shoes.

(3) Take with you pencils, rubber, highlighter pens, tissues, water, food, lip salve, throat sweets, and a mobile phone for emergencies. Make sure you know the name, address and telephone number of the studio you are going to.

(4) Plan to get there early – take the train *before* the last possible train. Get to the door of the studio at least 15 minutes before you are expected. Go for a walk for 10 minutes then ring the bell five minutes early.

(5) Switch off your mobile phone, pager, and digital watch.

(6) Be friendly and learn the names of everyone you are introduced to. If you find this difficult, go on a memory course. It is

important. One very famous voice artist carries a notebook so he can write down people's names and anything interesting they may tell him. Next time he meets them he not only knows their name but can refer to something they talked about last time. Needless to say he is universally liked and always working!

(7) Get hold of the script as soon as possible (without appearing too amateurishly eager) and retire to a quiet corner. Read it out loud. Try it in various ways and mark it up with pauses and inflections. One of the busiest London voice studios has fitted lecterns to the rear of the cubicle doors in the toilets so that one can study in peace and comfort.

(8) Back in the studio ask as many questions as possible before opening your mouth to start work. Find out what they want – who, how, what, when, where and why? Listen to the answers and if there are contradictions refrain from pointing them out. Nobody likes a wiseguy!

(9) Never criticise the script no matter how awful it is. The day you let rip with 'Who wrote this rubbish?' a small voice is bound to answer you with 'I did. And I also write the cheques, so get on with it!' Every script is somebody's baby and, like all babies, they love it.

(10) Most advertising scripts have been legally cleared and approved for broadcast before you see them. If they are changed they have to go through the clearance process again and the changes might not be acceptable. Don't change them. You are paid to read exactly what is put in front of you – no more, no less.

(11) If you are given confusing direction don't point this out. Smile and get on with it!

(12) Try not to be a victim of the situation. You have been booked as a professional who knows what he or she is doing and is doing something that the client can't do.

(13) If possible try to offer a choice of two good but slightly different takes so that you remove the fatal 'like it' or 'don't like it' choice. If you do your best and they don't like it, where do you go from there? If they have a choice of two there's a chance that one will be preferred and this is a starting point for discussion and experimentation.

(14) If it is a hard session and your energy levels drop, try jumping up and down on the spot. It may look stupid but it generates energy.

(15) Beware open mics in the booth. Do not mutter under your breath, sigh in exasperation, belch or break wind. Big brother is listening!

(16) Remember – the sole reason for doing any job is to get booked for another one. So do whatever it takes.
(17) If you want a copy of your work leave a blank DAT or cassette plus a stamped and addressed padded envelope.
(18) When the job is finished – leave! They have got other things to get on with. Thank everybody by name as you go.

Depending on the size and cost of the studio you have been working in you may have met the following people.

The Engineer

He (very often she) sits in the big chair in front of the desk. His job is to liaise between the voice artist in the booth and everyone else in the control room. His is the voice you are most likely to hear in the talkback. It is his job is to make your voice sound as good as possible and to ensure that it is safely recorded. He has absolute control over everything you hear in your cans. He can, should he so choose, make your working conditions very difficult and your voice sound horrible. A wise voice artist gets on well with the engineer.

The Tape-OP

He (or she) is the engineer's assistant. He may not operate the tape recorder as this is now easily under the control of the engineer, but he will change the mic position, plug in the headphones and other equipment, get tea, coffee, water and sandwiches, and unblock the toilet as and when necessary. He may be known as Teaboy, Runner or Gopher but really wants to be an engineer. He usually achieves his ambition. A wise voice artist gets on well with the tape-op.

The Producer

More commonly found in the USA than in the UK. He (or she) is the person who makes the ultimate decisions in artistic matters – unless overruled by either the creative director or the client. He may well give you 'line readings' which show you how the script should be phrased and inflected. He may try to explain the feelings and concepts behind the script. The words used may sound familiar but the way in which they are used will cause you to doubt your own mastery of the English/American language!

The Creative Director

He (or she) works for the advertising agency and is the person who makes the ultimate decisions in artistic matters, unless overruled by the client. He probably wrote the script. Again, he may well talk to you in a language you feel you ought to understand but which, for some strange reason, remains a mystery to you.

The Client

The Client is often there because it gives him (or her) an excuse to have a day away from work. He would like you to say much, much more than the creative director has written for you. The Client is the man who signs the cheque.

10

Radio Acting

Radio drama is a British invention and has been an essential part of British cultural life for over 75 years. It has been so popular and so successful that it is often referred to as the Second National Theatre of Great Britain. Some radio dramas, especially the fantasy adventure series, have attracted audiences of many millions, and proposals to reschedule a popular soap are likely to meet with public outcry. Radio drama survives and flourishes in Britain despite the all-pervading influence of television.

It has also been extremely popular in other countries, in particular the USA. Orson Welles' production of *The War Of The Worlds* attracted such large audiences who were so affected by it that an hysterical panic overcame large sections of the population. People began to evacuate cities and public service announcements were made to reassure the population that what they were listening to was a play and not reality! Such is the power of radio drama. Subsequently, the USA suffered an almost fatal decline in radio drama, but recent co-productions between the BBC and American stations have sowed the seeds of a fairly healthy revival.

THE REP

The BBC used to have a full-time company of actors called The Radio Drama Repertory Company, always known as 'The Rep'. Their job was to provide the cast for the weekly plays, appear as minor characters in the soaps and series, and read stories and poems as and when necessary. Jobs on the Rep were much prized and competition for places was fierce. Some open auditions were held, although most were 'by invitation' and potential recruits were expected to submit themselves for recorded workshop sessions which took place in radio drama studios. Contracts were usually for 18 months, employment (and wages) were guaranteed, and it was considered to be a prestigious job.

The Rep survived until the end of the 1990s. A new station controller and a new Head of radio drama were appointed at Radio 4, new policies formulated, and the members of the Rep were not replaced when their contracts ended. The BBC remained committed to a high drama output, however, and so the various acting jobs were placed on the open market rather than being cast from within the Rep. The BBC employs a great many drama directors in London, Manchester, Birmingham, Belfast, Cardiff, Glasgow and Edinburgh. They all produce and direct plays and so the actor wishing to work in radio has to be in contact with all of them. The BBC still holds some auditions but these are by invitation only. Directors usually like to see an actor working on stage before casting them, and they also like to have a radio drama tape so that they can hear how the voice sounds on mic. Actors are sometimes employed solely on the strength of a tape – especially if it is produced by someone known to the BBC drama department.

Recordings take place between 10am and 6pm so actors in shows are able to undertake radio engagements in the daytime.

There is a long-standing formula which is still regarded as the ideal format for a radio drama tape. Producers like to hear (although not in any specified order): a poem, a Shakespearean extract, a contemporary piece, and a comedy piece.

The poem should be short and complete – not an extract. It should not be *The Rime Of The Ancient Mariner* but it can be a sonnet – Shakespearean or otherwise. It can also be humorous.

Shakespeare is the actor's graveyard! Whatever you do somebody will judge you to have got it wrong. It is considered a mistake to launch yourself into an heroic harangue by one of the hero kings. If you are likely to be cast in one of those leading roles you will not be required to submit a tape – your work will already be familiar to the powers that be. The fees for radio plays are quite modest, especially for 'star' names, but most of them are only too pleased to be asked to appear. Directors have little difficulty in getting their preferred casts. Consequently, it is important to choose a piece of Shakespeare from a role that you might be considered for. There is no harm in recording 'The Queen is without, your majesty' or 'Yes, my liege' as they are the radio equivalents of 'spear carrying'!

A much preferred alternative, however, is to record a sonnet. These are 14 lines long, usually last one minute exactly, and have a beginning, a middle and an end. The problem is that they too can be very hard to get right. They do, however, cover a very wide range of emotions, attitudes, social positions and subjects. Because they are so well written and so intimate it can easily take two hours of well-directed studio time to get a satisfactory recording of a sonnet, however well prepared you are.

The contemporary piece is usually taken from the works of a living author. There are thousands of living authors whose work is produced on stage, TV and radio. Much of it is not suitable for radio audiences and it is not sensible to choose a piece which it was not possible to broadcast. The radio audience can be easily offended so sending in something peppered with lurid expletives would not demonstrate a familiarity with the relevant standards and conventions.

The comedy extract does not necessarily have to make the listener laugh out loud. A descriptive passage from a Dickens novel or a monologue from an Ayckbourn farce are both equally suitable.

CHOICE OF MATERIAL

It is important to strike a balance within the four pieces. It would be a mistake for both the comedy and the poem to be taken from the works of Shakespeare if the 'contemporary' was from *Shakespeare In Love*. Put these three with the compulsory Shakespeare and you have an all-Shakespeare audition tape. Between 1999 and 2000, BBC Radio 3, Radio 4, and BBC World Service collaborated on major productions of all the Shakespeare plays so they are unlikely to be producing them again in the near future. Recording one piece of Shakespeare is regarded as a good 'test'; recording four pieces might not see the applicant taken seriously!

Directors will want to hear the range of your voice – what is your natural pitch. When plays are being cast attention is paid to the range of pitches within the cast. Having two male leads with similarly pitched voices can confuse the listener. It is better to have one in the tenor register and one in the bass. If you have any 'mother tongue' regional accents you should choose pieces which show them off. Type casting is becoming more the norm but there are still openings for actors with genuine regional accents in addition to the standard RP. It is only in the fields of comedy and satire that a 'false' accent might be considered to be acceptable.

The pieces that you choose should be no longer than two minutes each. In the theatre it is a brave person who gets up and walks out of a production. In the comfort of a BBC director's suite, however, it is all too easy to reach for the off switch. In radio drama there is very little willing suspension of disbelief. An item on an audition tape has to make an immediate impact and then stop before the magic fades. The pieces chosen should be able to be 'dressed up' to sound as if they are extracts from actual productions. Try to find pieces that can be set somewhere, for example in a pub, a garden, by the sea, or in the street. Many scenes take place 'in the living room', but could there be some music or the radio or TV playing in the background? Can something be heard from outside – traffic, music, animals, wind, rain, children? BBC sound effects discs cover thousands of situations by providing what is called atmos or skyline. Atmos is a recording of the actual sounds heard in a particular location, while skyline is the silence heard in places such as the city at night or an empty cathedral. There is very little 'silence' in the world. Our ears filter out a lot of the background sounds in our environment. When we listen to a play or watch a film we expect them to be there and this time we 'hear' them – they are not filtered out. For an audition tape to sound authentic these background sounds should be included.

If you are in a bar do you have a sip from your drink or light a cigarette during you speech? Recording a speech with a pint glass in your hand completely changes the characterisation because it changes your body language – it usually makes actors sound more philosophical. As you bring the glass closer to the face it changes the actual sound of the voice. Some sci-fi voices are created by talking directly into a glass close to the microphone. Recording with an unlit cigarette between the lips also has a dramatic effect on the voice, and almost all listeners will know what is happening. If you do feel moved to strike a match or flick a lighter do not actually light the cigarette – most voice studios are non-smoking areas.

Assuming that you are in a bar and talking out loud, not to yourself, the question of exactly who you are talking to has to be addressed. How do you, as an actor, create the listener? This is your audition tape so getting someone else to say the odd line or do the odd off-mic grunt is not a good idea. They might upstage you, they might want to be paid, and they will certainly have a legal interest in your tape.

With modern recording technology it is very easy to create a 'two-hander', with one actor playing two (or more) parts. This is usually done as a series of drop-ins. the first speech from character 1 is recorded; this is replayed to the actor who then becomes character 2 and responds; these two speeches are replayed, the actor resumes his role as character 1, and reads the next speech. This process continues until the script is completed. The recording is then reviewed and any unsatisfactory parts can be rerecorded and replaced. This is usually done on a computer-based recording system using cut and paste techniques. With a highly skilled engineer it can also be achieved using Adats or even ¼″ tape where cut and paste becomes, quite literally, cut and splice.

Some actors prefer to record all the speeches from character 1 in one go, then record all the speeches from character 2, and then put them together in the correct sequence. This often sounds very wooden and artificial. With the drop-in method it is possible for the characters to talk under each other and to cough, sneeze, grunt or sigh while the other is speaking. This lends authenticity and tricks the listener into believing that there really are two actors in the scene. Creating a two-hander works best for comedy scripts. It takes an extremely skilled actor to play two parts convincingly in a serious scene. The human ear is very quick to see through a 'disguised' voice and the radio listener, not being distracted by costume, sets or lighting effects, is not easily fooled.

Some extracts only imply the presence of a third party. If your chosen character does not have many long passages it is possible, sometimes with a little rewriting, to join together several speeches to make a longer sequence. An actor for whom I was producing a radio drama tape read several speeches from one character, but left gaps in between each one. When I enquired what was happening in the gaps he replied, rather crossly, 'That's the other person speaking'! This approach does not work.

The accepted way of creating a non-existent person is to talk *to* them but not leave any gaps in which they could say anything. This requires a certain momentum in the delivery, and any pause should be preceded by a non-interrogative upward inflection. In the following example a man or woman, in their mid-40s, with a slightly downmarket accent, is talking to his/her friend in a wine bar.

(Wine bar atmos, musical wallpaper in background) This is on the CD.

I was talking to John the other night . . . you know him, he's the chap with the blue BMW, yes well, that would be nice just a white wine please, anyway he said that he was putting all his money into property. Now, obviously, I don't know what you do with your spare cash but I've always put mine into Unit Trusts. He thinks that the markets are going to collapse pretty soon so he's cashed everything in and bought himself a nice little house next to the University. Thanks, cheers! His son's girlfriend is doing chemistry up there and she says that they have terrible trouble finding enough places for the new students to stay. So, it's nice this Australian wine isn't it? Anyway he phoned the office and found out that they pay eighty five pounds a week for a room with shared kitchen and bathroom. So he's converting this house into five bedsits and that will bring him in over four hundred a week, that's twenty thousand a year! After paying the bills he reckons he's going to be left with about 15 grand spare – and that's enough for a mortgage on another place! Mind you, he always was good with money – his wife says he's got a slot across the top of his head!

(Laughter which dissolves into a fit of coughing. Fade)

This needs to be delivered in no more than 60 seconds, but ideally in only 50. It relies on momentum for effect. The speaker is in a good mood and punctuates his or her speech with chuckles and incredulous upward inflections. During the course of the story the speaker finishes one glass of wine, is offered another, accepts, tastes and approves, all without letting the other person get a word in!

This piece is a fine example of 'keeping all the balls in the air'. Just like the juggler – if one ball hits the floor the effect is ruined. One downward inflection would give the non-existent listener an opportunity to but in and, since non-existent people have nothing to say, we cease to 'believe' the speaker.

SHAKESPEARE

The previous script could qualify as either a 'modern' or a 'comedy'. In choosing a Shakespearean extract great care has to be taken in finding something which suits the playing age and weight of the voice. The chosen piece has to be examined in some detail – in this extract from *Henry VI* Part II, Queen Margaret, who is young and French, complains about both her situation and her disappointment in her husband – Henry VI.

> *My Lord of Suffolk, say, is this the guise,*
> *Is this the fashions in the court of England?*
> *Is this the government of Britain's isle,*
> *And this the royalty of Albion's king?*
> *What, shall King Henry be a pupil still,*
> *Under the surly Gloucester's governance?*
> *Am I a queen in title and in style,*
> *And must be made a subject to a duke?*
> *I tell thee, Pole, when in the city Tours*
> *Thou ran'st a tilt in honour of my love*
> *And stol'st away the ladies' hearts of France,*
> *I thought King Henry had resembled thee*
> *In courage, courtship, and proportion;*
> *But all his mind is bent to holiness,*
> *To number Ave-Maries on his beads;*
> *His champions are the prophets and apostles;*
> *His weapons, holy saws of sacred writ;*
> *His study is his tilt-yard, and his loves*
> *Are brazen images of canonized saints.*
> *I would the college of the Cardinals*
> *Would choose him Pope, and carry him to Rome,*
> *And set the triple crown upon his head;*
> *That were a state fit for his holiness.*

The stage direction is 'London – a room in the castle'. Castles tend to be made of stone and quite reverberant. This could be recorded against the sound of distant feet on stone floors with a small degree of reverb added to the voice. There is a very useful BBC sound effect (BBC CD SFX 004 track 5) which is a recording of the atmosphere in the National Gallery in London. If played at a low level behind a speech it sounds very much like distant people and footsteps in a castle. The speech could equally well be set in the palace gardens against the sounds of birds and perhaps children playing. There are no rules as directors can set plays and scenes wherever they please.

The Queen is young and French. Decisions have to be made as to the degree of her French accent. Is it slight, heavy, or non-existent? Her husband is Henry with a sounded 'h', but this name is pronounced 'onree' by the French. Governance would be 'goovernonce', while What sounds like 'water' and Champions like 'shompeeons'. Whatever decision is made there has to be consistency throughout. It is not really permissible to drop one 'h' and not the others – she is a Queen.

She is complaining to Suffolk, with whom she is in love, about what a disappointment her husband, the King, is to her. A dangerous situation. Would she be shouting or talking in conspiratorial tones? Radio is a wonderful medium for conspirators and lovers alike. On stage the actress has to produce enough volume and projection to hit the back wall of the theatre. In the radio studio she can be as intimate as she wishes. If this speech is done with anger it can be suppressed anger rather than explosive rage. Another option is to be quietly sarcastic.

> <u>His</u> champions are the prophets and apostles;
> His <u>weapons</u>, holy saws of sacred writ;
> His <u>study</u> is his tilt-yard, and his <u>loves</u>
> Are brazen images of <u>canonized saints</u>.

Make it clear that she much prefers Suffolk, who is more appealing in the areas of champions, weapons, study, and (best of all) love.

Any speech on a radio drama tape has to work without any reference to what may or may not have gone before. The listener, from whom you hope to get work, may not be a Shakespearean scholar. He or she may not even like Shakespeare. What they hear has to communicate and make sense away from its original context, and this has to be the primary concern when choosing and recording a Shakespearean piece. It may be necessary to sacrifice some of the poetry or even the metre in order to make it work. The punctuation, which in the above extract dates from the 19th century, can be confusing. Shakespeare did not necessarily write with punctuation as we know it, and sometimes it is better ignored. It is your voice and your communication skills that are being assessed – not Shakespeare!

Recording Shakespeare is a dangerous operation – as is writing about the recording of it! Whatever you do or say will always be criticised by some and praised by others. A safer Shakespearean option is to record a sonnet.

Shakespearean Sonnets

Sonnet 130 lends itself to imaginative interpretation. The accepted reading is that of a sighing man in love with a slightly (for the time and convention) unusual woman – dark skinned and dark haired. Sonnets are generally assumed to have been written to be read rather than said. They are ideal for radio as they can be delivered as 'internalisations' – thoughts taking place in the speaker's head. This one, however, could be one half of a conversation. Imagine two north country servants, a summer Sunday afternoon, and a country tavern. The two boys have had a few pots of ale and they are sitting outside on the banks of the mill stream. The sun and the ale have combined to create a relaxed, contemplative atmosphere. One bemoans his working conditions and goes in to some detail about the unpleasant character of his employer's wife. He then turns to the other and says something like, 'What's your mistress like?' The reply he gets is:

My mistress' eyes are nothing like the sun	1
Coral is far more red than her lips' red;	
If snow be white, why then her breasts are dun;	
If hairs be wires, black wires grow on her head;	4
I have seen roses damasked, red and white,	
But no such roses see I in her cheeks;	6
And in some perfumes is there more delight	
Than in the breath that from my mistress reeks.	8
I love to hear her speak, yet well I know	
That music hath a far more pleasing sound;	10
I grant I never saw a goddess go;	
My mistress when she walks treads on the ground.	12
And yet, by heaven, I think my love as rare	
As any she belied with false compare.	

The second boy tells us that his mistress is dull eyed, pale lipped, dark skinned, dark haired, sallow of lip and complexion, suffering from bad breath, possessed of a grating voice, and overweight. Despite all this he is infatuated with her – or is it the beer talking?

Performed with a northern English accent (slightly tipsy) and set against a backdrop of running water and summer birds, this sonnet takes on a whole new meaning.

Sonnet 12, supposedly so placed to reflect the time element in its first line, can also be made to tell an interesting story. We hear the sound of a softly crackling wood fire with the gentle ticking of a clock in the background. The speaker is a woman who is deciding to dispense with the services of her lover. She conjures up a picture of him and notes the degeneration of his former charms – the 'violet' past prime with the greying of the attendant foliage, the lofty 'tree' now barren. Her voice is low and husky, she is clearly a sexually orientated creature, we may even hear the gentle rustle of sheets. She sprinkles her delivery with significant inuendic pauses and line 10 makes it very clear that she, or old father time, is sending him away.

The final couplet clearly states the nature of her favourite pastime – 'nothing' in Shakespeare is sometimes used as a euphemism for the female organ necessary to the procreation of the species and the consequent outwitting of the grim reaper.

When I do count the clock that tells the time,	*1*
And see the brave day sunk in hideous night;	
When I behold the violet past prime,	
And sable curls all silvered o'er with white:	*4*
When lofty trees I see barren of leaves,	
Which erst from heat did canopy the herd,	*6*
And summer's green all girded up in sheaves	
Borne on the bier with white and bristly beard:	*8*
Then of thy beauty do I question make,	
That thou among the wastes of time must go,	*10*
Since sweets and beauties do themselves forsake,	
And die as fast as they see others grow,	*12*
And nothing 'gainst time's scythe can make defence	
Save breed to brave him, when he takes thee hence.	

A Modern Piece

This is a modern piece from *Steaming* by Nell Dun. In the play the speaker, Josie, is in her mid-30s, a Londoner, and working in a disreputable club. She is talking to Nancy who enjoys a rather better situation in life. It is important to work out which 'you' refers specifically to Nancy and which is used in more general terms. Attention to details like these help the listener to believe the illusion that Nancy is really there.

They are in a Turkish bath. This piece can be recorded with the background sounds of a Turkish bath and with reverberation on the voice. However, it is such a well-written speech that (for the purposes of a radio audition tape) Josie can be any age, any accent, and anywhere. The speech has to work away from the original context. Josie obviously feels what she is saying passionately and might be upset by the end of the speech. In radio, the passion has to be controlled as yelling and shouting do not work and will probably cause the listener, from whom you want work, to switch the tape off. The required effect can be created by introducing tension into the body and speaking quite quietly close to the microphone.

Do not get carried away – stay in control!

What sort of a job can I get? I'm not even a young girl any more. And I happen to like nice things ... I like money ... I don't like wearing 'sensible' shoes and last year's coat and organising other people's lives like a colonel-in-chief. Well, I'm going to tell you something – I don't want to be like you. It's boring, it's every day! Boring! Boring! Boring! Do you know why us working-class women have a little bit on the side? Why we spend money on clothes and make-up and shoes when we don't, as you say, 'strictly need them'? We've been brought up to do the shit work and we can't escape from doing the shit work except by finding a man with money and hanging on to him! Anyway, who's to say you've got a better life than me? – I'm not so sure – I've been to South Africa, Barbados, Tenerife – I've laid beside more pools than you've had hot dinners!

You don't thieve because you don't need to, not because you're any better than I am! I want excitement in my life! I want beautiful clothes, beautiful travelling, cars ... if I've got to steal them – well, at least I've had them, which is more than I can say for you. Have your drab dreary life and keep your good name if that's what you want. Women should be beautiful things of pleasure. Do you know what it feels like to go into a library if you don't know your way around ... and you get looked down on because of your accent? ... It's a horrible feeling being looked down on – being turned down for job after job because you haven't got the qualifications ... because you can't spell and you can't speak right ... and you know in the end all they're going to offer you is cleaning!

The Poem
The choice of poem needs careful consideration. It should contrast with the other material on the tape. If you have recorded a dreamy, romantic sonnet as the Shakespeare then the poem might benefit from being humorous. If all the other material has been light-hearted, the poem should be serious. It could be a sonnet (Shakespearean or not), or it could be as simple as this from John Donne:

Song

Stay, oh sweet, and do not rise,
The light that shines comes from thine eyes;
The day breaks not, it is my heart,
Because that thou and I must part.
Stay, or else my joys will die,
And perish in their infancie.

Once the stresses and inflections have been sorted out all that remains is the problem of the last couplet. It does not rhyme in modern English, and, like some Shakespeare, the only way to make it rhyme is to read it with an English Midlands accent.

A poem like this is often best recorded without music, sound effects or atmosphere. It should have a feeling of intimacy, as if the speaker is thinking it rather than saying it. This is best achieved by speaking quietly, quite close to the microphone. There are, of course, exceptions. This, *The Highwayman* by Paul Bura, might benefit from some moorland atmosphere, the approach of a galloping horse, and a few distant owls:

The Highwayman came riding
Over the misty moor
He'd had his oats In John O'Groats
And was riding back for more!

When choosing and recording a poem do not be afraid to do something as simple as this – complete with sound effects. If you can make the listener smile both at the poem and at your mastery of the medium of radio, you are more likely to be employed.

RADIO DRAMA STUDIOS

Radio drama studios are very different from voice-over studios. The biggest difference is in the size. Drama studios are usually fairly big – 12 metres by 7 metres is not unusual – and they often have very high ceilings. A good radio drama studio can function like a theatrical set, with different areas for different parts of the action. Directors build these in the studio using screens (both reflective and non-reflective), curtains and furniture. The studio will contain a large 'live' area with a wooden floor, and a 'dead' area with heavy carpet and soundproofing curtains. The live area is used for indoor scenes where there are sound reflections off walls, doors and floors. This area of the studio will often contain a flight of stairs going up to the ceiling. One side of the treads will be carpeted, the other will be bare wood. This gives two acoustically different stair sounds and the actors will be required to make their exits and entrances,

171

if the script calls for it, using these dummy stairs. There will be a variety of doors and windows with different locks, bolts, chains, knockers, letterboxes, bells and buzzers for use in the production.

The dead area is used for outside scenes where there is no reflective acoustic. If you listen carefully to radio drama you can 'hear' the room in which it is set. This is deliberate; a scene in a car sounds different from a scene in a cathedral. Voice-over studios, on the other hand, go to great lengths to eliminate all sounds of being in a room. Early radio drama now sounds very artificial because it was usually a group of actors bunched around one microphone in a large reverberant studio. Their 'outdoor' scenes never sounded very convincing – wind or a light breeze was provided by means of a hand-cranked machine in the corner of the studio. Nowadays it is played into the scene from a sound effects CD, usually during the post-production stage so the actors don't hear the effects they are working with. It is extremely unusual for radio actors to wear headphones. It is also extremely unusual for them to receive playback – they seldom know what a scene sounds like. The director makes all the decisions and the actors, usually, do what they are told. Radio drama productions are highly organised affairs with each actor being booked for the minimum time possible in order to save money. The BBC expects to record 30 minutes of drama in a 10am to 6pm day with a one-hour lunch break. Not all actors called for a particular day will be working all the time so there is usually a greenroom in which they can relax.

Radio personnel have slightly different jobs from those in the voice-over world, and some of them have the same jobs but different job titles.

The Director
The director is in complete charge and is answerable to no-one else in the studio. His (or her) 'client' is the commissioning editor or Head of drama, and they are seldom seen in a studio. When the production is finished he will submit it to his superiors before it is broadcast and then they will have their say – usually when it is too late to change anything! The director is also the producer; as well as making all the major artistic decisions he will have decided on the play, the cast, the composer, the adapter, and the studio. He may also choose the technical team who work with him. He will certainly be responsible for the budget and the way it is spent.

The BA (Broadcast Assistant)
The BA is his assistant. She (or he) is usually a trained secretary but it would be a mistake to cast her only in this role. It is a highly skilled and responsible job and one which allows her to wield

considerable influence – especially in casting decisions. Make friends with the BA! She prepares the script for distribution to the cast, advises the director on the availability and cost of individual actors, makes casting suggestions if necessary, liaises with the contracts department, and prepares the budget. In the studio she keeps a log of all takes, mistakes, and out takes. She times every individual take and scene and generally cools the fevered brows of the creative team.

The Studio Manager

The studio manager is at least the equivalent of the engineer in the voice-over studio. She (or he) can have a huge artistic input into a production or they can confine themselves to making sure everything is recorded correctly. They work the 'panel', which is the BBC word for a desk.

SM Grams

Another archaic BBC job title still in use. The SM grams assists the SM panel in the cubicle by playing in the sound effects and music discs. Historically, these were played on a gramophone – hence 'grams'. Nowadays, they are usually on CD, sometimes on DAT or tape, and hardly ever on disc.

SM Spot

The SM spot works in the studio with the actors. She (or he) will be asked to move mics and props, but her main function will be to provide the live sound effects which accompany the action. These might be pouring tea, drawing a sword, using tools, using a knife and fork – almost anything you can imagine. These can be performed on a special 'spot' mic or on the actor's mic. This entails working very physically close to the actor. Radio scripts are stapled at the top left-hand corner only and are held in the right hand, the pages being silently turned by the left. The actor has his hands full and cannot manage props without courting disaster. Drinking is about as much as is possible, and even then the SM spot will probably hand it to, and take it from, them.

FINDING WORK

Radio drama directors are keen to employ actors with a love of the medium and they will try to find out if you listen to the output and know what is going on in their world. It is a good idea to tape record as much of the output as possible and listen to at least some of each production. The closing credits can be a mine of information. You need to build up a database of everything relating to radio drama. Some productions are made within the BBC, while some are made by independent production companies; most of these are run by, or employ, ex-BBC people.

For BBC productions, the most useful point of contact is the BA. If you call the BBC switchboard and ask to be put through to a particular director you will probably be put through to his office and will end up speaking to his BA. The only way to get directly to a director is to know, and ask for, his extension number. BBC switchboard operators are highly skilled in detecting and diverting callers who don't quite know their way around the BBC. If you do know an extension number it is possible to dial it direct, providing you prefix it with the 'other' BBC exchange number.

BAs can be very helpful. They might tell you about forthcoming productions, or you might be able to persuade them to put your photo, tape and CV on a director's desk. They might even be kind enough to suggest you for a minor part.

Independent production companies working outside of the BBC engage their artistic and technical teams for each production as and when they need them. They might not make casting decisions themselves unless they have suggested a package to the BBC which included a star name. Most independent companies use the same directors as much as they can – providing, of course, they are making successful productions. Nearly all of these directors are ex-BBC so it might be possible to get their contact details from one of the friendly BAs at Broadcasting House.

There are opportunities for actors other than from the drama departments. *The Archers* is produced and recorded in Birmingham. They introduce new characters into the series at regular intervals and keep records of actors who send them their details and tapes. However, they will only cast someone who is right for the part rather than create a part for someone who is right for the series. Keeping in touch with the BA in the production office might alert you to planned auditions. They also use some freelance directors so it is as well to keep a list of these and try to find out their contact details.

BBC World Service Drama has now been integrated with the Drama Department in Broadcasting House, but a series known as English By Radio still maintains a company of actors at the World Service headquarters in Bush House. The series, known in the trade as 'E by R', is used to teach the English language through the medium of radio drama. There are dramatised stories and mini-soaps which are discussed and dissected by the on-air teaching staff.

Short story, story and poetry readings are not produced by the Drama Department. they have their own producers and departments. Again, it is necessary to listen to find out who is doing what.

Some of the departments are not in London but have been devolved to the regions. The producers like to hear material relevant to their particular field – a poetry producer should be sent at least a poem and a sonnet. A short story producer should be sent something modern and something classical, with one of them containing a few different character voices.

On-air continuity is a self-contained department which usually employs people who have been actors. They look for clear speaking voices with a sound and style suitable for each station. Radio 3 is more serious in its approach than Radio 2; Radio 4 lies somewhere in between the two. They will listen to tapes but they do hold auditions and have their own training programmes. Television stations and channels also have continuity departments, and most have a house style which changes according to fashion or the whim of the controller. BBC TV advertise continuity vacancies from time to time and ask all applicants to record a specific audition tape. The likely brief is: 'Choose your six favourite television programmes, introduce them, in one minute, in the style of either BBC 1 or BBC2, and say which one.' The 'trap' is in the timing. You are expected to introduce all six in the space of one minute – not take one minute for each. Continuity announcers are expected to have scriptwriting skills and, when things go wrong, nerves of steel! There is a continuity script in chapter 4.

Trails and promos are on-air publicity and deal with programmes which will be shown in the near or not so near future. They are rather like voice-overs in that the voice, style, and approach are dependent on the programme being trailed or promoted. Sometimes they use dark brown chocolatey voices and sometimes whacky characters. Most stations have in-house producers who specialise in this area and they will listen to tapes demonstrating the necessary skills.

The BBC have an in-house magazine called *Aerial* in which most staff vacancies and some freelance opportunities are advertised. These include voice jobs. *Aerial* is distributed within the BBC but is also available on subscription to people on the outside. Details can be found on the BBC website, where there are also some job vacancies and many programme scripts and transcripts – a very useful source of material.

All programme makers maintain a list of readers who can be called on to read letters, documents, statements, extracts, English translations, and listeners' letters. Some directors prefer letters to be read by non-professional voices chosen from, for example, the typing pool. They feel that this makes them sound more 'authentic'.

11

The Wrap

If you have worked on all the scripts in this book and tried to perform them in the suggested ways you will have learned something of the power of subtlety. The 'tunes' we use in speech are a more effective form of communication than the words that go with them. The tune tells the listener how to 'see' and hear what you are saying. Say the words 'I'm really happy' to the tune more normally associated with 'I'm really fed up' and the message of the tune is the one that will be believed.

The response of the listener is very much under the control of the voice-over artist. This response is triggered not by 'what' is said but by the 'way' it is said. We have the power to tell people how to respond to what we are saying. Consequently, all scripts and messages must be delivered in a positive manner, no matter how ill or miserable you might be feeling. The negative thoughts and feelings of the voice artist are all too easily communicated to the listener and they will obviously detract from the message or product.

I have stressed the importance of the 'rising inflection'. It is one of the hardest voice-over techniques to master and some people find it almost impossible. However, some directors will not want rising inflections. Commercials aimed at teenagers often underplay the script and go for a 'couldn't care less if you buy it or not' delivery. If you have a young sounding voice it is important to be able to give this completely unenthusiastic read. It is surprisingly easy to do! However, to be successful, the voice-over artist must be able to pitch his or her voice wherever the director wants it to be – rising or falling. Being known as a 'one read voice' restricts your chances of work.

Most people find falling inflections to be negative, and descending pitch patterns switch them off – they stop listening. In the hands of an experienced professional the rising inflection may hardly be noticed, but it will be there. The pitch change may only be very small but the listener will 'hear' it as a positive message.

Positive body language and posture will help to create the necessary positive attitude. Always stand when you are recording – it really does sound and feel a lot better than if you are slumped in a chair. Use your hands, move your head, and smile! You don't have to mean it – just do it!

You tell your listener how to respond to your message. This is as true in everyday life as it is in the make-believe reality of voice-over. For example, what about *your* message? What about the message that *you* give to prospective employers when you go in search of work? Is that going to be negative or positive? Are you expecting to be rejected? Would rejection be a comforting confirmation of your own opinion of yourself? Are you going to hide behind the impersonality of the 'Dear Sir or Madam' letter and the unsolicited Jiffy Bag?

Sending out unsolicited tapes does not work. Personal contact does – as long as you project a positive image. Find out exactly who you need to speak to in a particular organisation and then write a script covering all the points you want to make. Practise the script standing up, with a telephone clamped to your ear, and using the name of the person you will be speaking to. Call them when you are feeling confident but keep the script in your hand – it will save you from getting tongue-tied and forgetting what it is that you want to say.

Here is a useful script:

Hello, Miss Wheeler, my name's Warrington Minge and I'm a voice-over artist. I've just put together a new voice tape and I'm about to send you a copy. Now, I've got rather a lot of material – I know how busy you are, I don't want to waste your time – what would you like to hear? I've got some very sexy soft sell, a few hard hitting furniture ads, a couple of comic characters (chuckle), and some Blue Chip corporate work. What are you casting at the moment? What would you like me to put on your tape?

Very few people are quick witted enough to say 'Silence' or 'A $50 bill'! But if they do you might well make a lasting impression on them by complying with their request! Send the real tape a couple of days later! If they do manage to decline your offer then the door remains open for you to contact them again in a month's time.

The letter you send with the tape could read something like this:

Dear Miss Wheeler
Further to our conversation I have pleasure in enclosing, as requested, my voice tape. You said that you'd like to hear

something sexy so I've sent you three commercials – Black
Magic, Bombay Sapphire, and Black Gold.
Thank you for your interest – I look forward to hearing from
you.
Best wishes
Warrington Minge.

If this letter is opened by a secretary the *enclosing as requested* phrase will ensure that he or she gives it to their boss rather than throwing it in the bin. Using this approach you will completely change the usual sales dynamic by getting the prospective employer to appear to ask you to send them your details.

Everything you send out should be presented to the highest possible standard. Use a word processor and print on good quality paper. Every letter should be personalised – take the time and trouble to find out exactly who you need to write to, get their correct address, and make sure you spell their name accurately. One large London agency guarantees to listen to all tapes except those accompanied by a 'Dear Sir or Madam' letter – they go straight in the bin. They say 'If you can't be bothered to find out about us then we can't be bothered to find out about you!'

Newcomers to the voice-over world often feel embarrassed by not having a voice-over CV, especially when advertising agencies ask them what they have done in the past. Sometimes the advertisers prefer to have voices which have not previously been associated with products. If an agency is casting a commercial for Ford cars, they are more likely to consider a beginner than someone who has just voiced a world-wide campaign for Volkswagen. The best policy is to present a completely honest CV. The advertising world is a small one and any 'economies of truth' are sure to be found out. Not having done any previous work can be as attractive a proposition as a CV littered with campaigns for world-famous brands.

It has often been said that the largest proportion of human effort is expended in the maintenance of the status quo. People don't like change – they prefer things to stay just the way they are. If a voice agent or casting director does not have you on his or her books they are likely to put more energy into keeping you off them than into giving you the chance to prove yourself. You will have to keep knocking on doors until finally you find one that is open to you. Learn to see rejection as a positive event. All it means is that you were not considered suitable for a particular job, or that your voice was similar to those already being represented by an agency or management. In six months time you may be exactly what they will be looking for. Getting work is a function of effort – sitting in a comfortable chair and moaning about the state of the business and the general lack of work will not get you employed. Calling people, reading all the trade papers, and sending out precisely targeted tapes will get results – sooner or later. Providing you are putting out energy, something will come back to you. It always does, even though it may be from a completely unexpected source. Keep working hard at promoting yourself and making contacts. It will make you feel and sound positive and you will have the confidence of someone who is 'in the market place'. You will be taking control of your career and not just sitting back and being a victim. When you do get the phone call for 'the big one' you will be in the right frame of mind to make the most of it.

Success in voice-over requires a lot of persistence – it is a very competitive business, in which good people do good work for good money. Unlike acting you will never be expected to 'pay to play' so don't offer to work for reduced fees – nobody will respect you for it. It is a fact of life that when 'the big one' comes along it is never given to someone who has cut their prices or performed favours. It always goes to someone who is seen as being professional.

I started this book by saying, 'It isn't what you've got – it's what you do with it that counts!' I'm going to end it by quoting a line from a song: 'It ain't what you say, it's the way that you say it – that's what gets results!'

12

Glossary of Terms

Acoustic	The modification of a sound by a room or space. Some rooms echo, some do not.
Adat	A tape-based digital recorder.
Added Value Words	Words such as plus, free, new, improved, and extra, which give the impression you are getting more than you have paid for. Words like and, but, so, and now, can also be added value words depending on the context.
ADR	Additional dialogue replacement. Recording and creating the speech and sounds made by background actors in a scene, including battle cries, screams, and non-specific conversation. Can also include performing scripted material for specific on screen characters. Known as 'looping' in the USA.
Advertising Agency	Works on behalf of a client and their product. Thinks up creative ideas – like 10 new ways to spend the advertising budget.
AFTRA	The American Federation of Radio and Television Artists. American union representing voice artists.
Agent	Someone who attempts to provide actors with work, and charges 15 per cent for the trouble.
Airtime	The length of a commercial and the number of times it is transmitted. Also refers to the amount of money that advertisers have to pay radio or TV stations to broadcast the commercial.
Ambience	The background sound of a place, location, or happening. Usually taken from a sound effects disc.
Analogue	An old-fashioned method of processing and tape recording sounds. It uses tapes and valves rather than computers. When everybody has bought computer systems this will become fashionable again.

Announcer Tag	The last few words of a commercial which are said by a different and more formal voice than the main.
Atmos	The BBC word for 'atmosphere'. Those who have escaped from the BBC now prefer to call it ambience.
Awareness Advertising	Advertisements from companies who are either so successful or have such an unbreakable monopoly that they have no need to advertise. Waterboards and electricity companies do use awareness advertising.
BA (Broadcast Assistant)	See 'PA(II)'.
Bass	Low frequency sounds, such as produced by a double bass.
BBC	The British Broadcasting Corporation – a group of radio and TV channels in the UK that only take advertisements from themselves.
Board	A North American term for a mixing desk.
Booth	A small padded room with a heavy door, especially designed for voice-over artists.
Busk	To make something up as you go along – voice artists and actors are sometimes asked to do this for background chatter effects.
Buy-out	A once and for all payment which precludes further payments for repeats or residuals.
Cans	Headphones – they relay sound directly to your ears.
Cassette	A small tape capable of recording and replaying poor quality sound.
Casting Director	The person who chooses who the director gets to choose from.
CD Burner	A machine which uses a laser to make CDs.
CD Rom	A CD which carries a computer programme.
Character	A voice, with personality, which is unlikely to be heard reading the news on the BBC.
Chest Voice	Using the resonant cavities of the chest when speaking.
Client	He (or she) who pays for it all. The one person in a recording studio who genuinely does not realise how unwelcome they are.
Clip	A short extract from an audio or video programme.
Close Miked	A microphone placed very close to the source of sound.
Closed	A mic which is not live is sometimes said to be closed.

Codec	The coder/decoder which converts analogue mic signals into digital signals which are transmitted down telephone lines. ISDN systems need a codec. The best codecs are now based within a computer.
Commercial Producer	The radio station employee who creates expensive sounding radio commercials and produces them as cheaply as possible. They decide which voice artist to book if they think it's becoming noticeable that they've already voiced most of this week's commercials themselves.
Compression	Squashing loud sounds and boosting quiet ones until they all appear to be at the same volume.
Continuity	The BBC radio and TV department which makes the announcements in between programmes. These are the people who don't panic when everything goes wrong. They say, 'And now let's listen to some music.' When the time signal fails to work they bang a glass or a lampshade with a pencil.
Control Room	Where everybody else sits, chats, laughs, and drinks tea, while the voice artist is locked up in his soundproofed booth.
Copy	The words that are known as the script.
Crashing	The sound of a voice artist who couldn't get all the words out before the jingle started.
Creative Director	It's their fault – the script, the concept, the music, the choice of studio, the fee, the voice-artist, the sandwiches …
Cubase	Software for recording with computers. Mostly used in music studios.
Cubicle	The BBC word for a control room because it used to only be big enough for the engineer and his equipment. There was no room for clients.
Cue	The word, sound, light, or movement after which you start.
Cue Light	The light which signals that it is time to start.
Cut and Paste	Moving sounds around in a computer and assembling a perfect recording from a series of imperfect ones.
Cut and Splice	Doing Cut and Paste with recording tape, a razor blade, a white chinagraph pencil, and small pieces of splicing tape. It is a highly skilled job now no longer required – until the computer crashes!
DAT	DAT is the industry standard mastering format. The tapes are small, contain digital information and can hold up to two hours of stereo sound.
Dead	As in not working, this is a dead microphone.

182

De-esser	A piece of outboard equipment capable of removing excess sibilance.
Demo Tape	An audio cassette which demonstrates what you could do if only someone would give you the chance. Professionals have a voice tape.
Desk	The mixing desk in the control room.
Diaphragm	The sensitive part of the microphone that picks up the sound, or the muscular part of the body that helps push the air out of the lungs thus creating the sound.
Digital	Sound is converted into electrical impulses which are then converted to digital information – a very fast stream of electrical ons and offs.
Director	The person making the final artistic decisions.
Directional	Some microphones are directional – they only pick up sound in one or two specified directions. Others pick up anything going.
Donut	An announcement or message which occurs in the middle of a commercial and which is performed by a voice other than the one which starts and ends it. This is an American term.
Drop-in	A previously recorded performance is replayed, and at an agreed point the system is put into record and the performer replaces part of the previous recording with yet another attempt to get the rest of it right.
Dubbing	Replacing the recorded voice on a film or video soundtrack. Can be done by the original actor or a completely different person.
Ducking Compressor	A backing track and a voice track are fed to a ducking compressor. Every time the voice says something the compressor turns down the volume of the backing or, sometimes mercifully, the other way round.
Duplicator	A machine capable of making several simultaneous copies of a cassette or CD.
Echo	The effect produced when sound bounces off a distant object.
Effects	Ways in which a sound can be changed or modified by the addition of echo, reverb, compression, flanging, gating, etc.
Elide	To run one word into another.
Emphasise	To give one or more words added importance by increasing their pitch or volume. Emphasis can also be created by pausing either before or after a word.
Engineer	The person in the control room who is in charge of the sound and the recording.
Equity	The British union representing voice artists.

Facility Houses	A recording, design, film or photographic studio which can be hired for short periods of time.
Fader	A slider on the recording desk which changes the volume of something being recorded or replayed.
Feedback	A nasty whistling sound caused when a microphone listens to it's own output.
Fishtank Effect	The paranoia experienced by a voice artist in their completely soundproofed booth when gazing out on a control room full of people.
Foldback	Foldback allows the voice artist to hear their own voice and any music and effects they might be working with.
Frequency Response	The measuring of the lowest and highest sound that a microphone, loudspeaker, or other equipment can reproduce.
Front	The start of a script or recording. Also known as the 'top'.
FX	Sound effects.
Gig	A slang term for a professional engagement.
Gopher	Employed to gopher anything that anybody needs. Is not usually allowed to be a part of the pecking order.
Grams	The BBC word for music or sound effects being provided from a pre-recorded medium.
Greenroom	A place where actors go to relax with one another.
Hard Sell	The approach beloved of furniture warehouses the world over – 'I'll stop shouting when you start buying'!
Harmoniser	Also known as the Munchkiniser. A piece of electronic equipment especially designed to change the pitch of the voice – usually upwards.
Headphones	Used to listen to the foldback – sounds played directly into the ear so that it is not picked up by the mic. Also known as cans.
Headset	A set of headphones which also have a microphone attached to them.
Head Voice	Using the resonant chambers of the head when speaking.
Howlround	The BBC word for feedback.
Ident	A recording made by the engineer which precedes the recording made by you. It will give the script title, artist's name and take number. You may be asked to do this yourself.

Improvise	To make something up as you go along – sometimes with another actor. This may be asked for at auditions for commercials. Cynics see it as a way of getting good ideas for free.
Inflection	A way of altering or reinforcing the meaning of a word by changing the way it is said.
Inlay Card	The folded information-bearing card that falls out of an audio cassette box.
ISDN	Integrated Services Digital Network is the system used to send digital information from one sound studio to another. Also used to send the voice from a voice-over's home studio to a recording studio or radio station.
Iso-booth	Another name for a booth.
Isolate	To emphasise a word by leaving a small gap both before and after it.
J Card	Another name for the information-bearing card that falls out of an audio cassette box.
Jewel Case	The impossible to open box that CDs live in.
Jiffy Bag	The padded envelope used to send CDs and tapes through the post. If you take yourself seriously use a new one every time.
Jingle	The music and singing specially composed for a particular commercial.
Legato	Smoothly.
Leave Them Hanging	Do not indicate the end of a thought or script by going down.
Level	The studio word for volume.
Library Music	Music which is written and recorded on spec and which is given away to production companies who only pay when they use it. It spends most of its life in libraries, waiting to be used.
Lift	Emphasising a word by lifting the pitch higher than the word either side of it.
Light	Keep it light – not too serious.
Limiter	A piece of equipment which stops any sound exceeding a certain level.
Line Reading	Explaining to a voice artist how you want a line to sound by demonstrating it yourself.
Live	A mic which is on.
Lock-up	When two or more recording machines or computers are running together.
Looping	Creating and recording the background speech noises and sound effects for film and television shows. There are groups of actors who regularly work together in this field.

Master	The original recording – not a copy
Mic	Microphone.
Mid	Sound which is between high frequency and low frequency.
Miked-Up	A microphone has been applied to the sound source in question.
Mixing Desk	The control panel in the control room where all the sound levels are set.
Monitors	The loudspeakers in the control room through which the sound is listened to.
Mono	Not stereo – exactly the same sound is coming from both speakers.
Mood Music	Another name for Library Music.
Moving On	When you have not responded to an availability check for work the booker will send you a message that, in view of your lack of response, she has moved on. You've lost the offer of the job! Can also mean that one script on a session has been recorded satisfactorily and it is time to move on to the next script.
Multitrack	A recording machine which is capable of recording or replaying several different tracks in parallel.
Music Bed	The music and or singing that goes with or under a commercial.
Nearfield	Monitors designed to be listened to at close quarters.
Newsreader	A person employed to read the news in a serious tone of voice.
Newscaster	A person employed to deliver the news without a serious tone of voice.
Off Line	A trial editing process which does not use expensive equipment.
Off-Mic	Sound being directed to an insensitive part of the mic.
On-Air	Something being broadcast live.
On-Mic	Sound being directed to the sensitive part of the mic.
Outboard	Equipment used to modify a recorded sound which is only brought into action when it is needed.
Over-run	The speech taking longer than it should or exceeding the length of the music.
PA (I)	Public address system. Also known as a Tannoy.
PA (II) (now known as BA)	The assistant to the director. She (or he) has specialist skills necessary in the recording environment.

Pack Shot	The picture of the product which usually ends a commercial.
Panel	The BBC name for the mixing desk.
Patched-In	An American way of saying that a voice is being relayed from a studio other than the one in which it is being recorded.
Phantom Power	The electricity fed to a voice-over mic – without which it will not work.
Pick-up	The American expression for a drop-in.
Pillow talk	The very sexy and intimate 'voice on the pillow'.
Playback	To hear your finished recording.
Plosives	The 'p' and 'b' sounds which cause a mic to 'pop'.
Pop Screen	A stretched gauze which sometimes prevents plosives from reaching the mic. Also known as a 'Pop Shield' or 'Popper Stopper'.
Popping	Plosives cause an explosion of air which causes the mic diaphragm to produce a 'pop' sound.
Positive Negative	A phrase which would have negative connotations outside of the commercial script but which is used to positive effect within the commercial.
Pre-amp	The electronics which amplify the signal from the mic before sending it to the desk or recorder.
Print Through	When recording tape is stored untouched for long periods of time, loud sounds can be partially transferred from one layer of tape to the one above. Consequently, you get a pre-echo of something before actually hearing it.
Pro Tools	A professional computer-based editing system for sound and vision.
Processors	Outboard equipment brought into play as and when it is needed.
Producer	The person making the final financial decisions.
Production Music	The American name for Library Music.
Promo	A short film made to advertise a film at a cinema – near you, now!
Proximity Effect	The extra bass sound generated when you speak very close to the microphone.
Read	The performance style of a script.
Real Person	Someone (usually a real person) pretending to be a real person and not a thespian. Real people are often found in commercials for pet food, washing powder and hair care products.
Real-time	An event taking as long as it actually takes.
Remote Studio	A studio containing a voice artist which is some distance from the one in which his or her performance is being recorded or from which it is being directed.

187

Repeats	When a broadcast programme is repeated, a percentage of the original performance fee eventually finds its way to the performer.
Replay	Hearing your recorded performance replayed to you.
Residuals	A percentage of the original fee paid after every block of six showings of a TV commercial – unless you accepted a 'buy-out' fee.
Retake	An attempt to improve on an existing recording by doing it again.
Reverb	The effect of sound bouncing round a space too small to produce a decent echo.
Route	The electronic channelling of sound within a mixing desk so that it arrives at a predetermined point.
RP	Received Pronunciation. The English habit of talking with a stiff upper lip.
Runner	The lowest of the low in the film and studio industry. The runner pecks last!
SAG	The Screen Actors Guild. American union representing voice artists.
Sadie	A professional computer-based sound editing system favoured by the BBC. Everybody else uses Pro Tools.
School talk	A rather authoritative delivery.
Session	The time arranged for and allocated to an audio recording. A recording engagement is also known as a session. The BBC call it a 'studio'.
SFX	Sound effects, live or recorded.
Shot Mute	Filmed without sound being recorded.
Shouters	The men who sell furniture and tabloid newspapers.
Showreel	A visual compilation of previous work which shows some of the things you can do – and none of the things that you can't!
Signal	The technical term for the flow of electricity representing sound.
Signal Chain	The path taken by the signal and the order in which it passes through various pieces of equipment.
Skyline	The sound of silence! Sound effects recordings of the 'silence' of, for example, the city at night, the countryside, or an empty church.
Slate	The recorded announcement which precedes a recording or each of a series of recordings of the same script.
Soft Sell	A way of selling using the gentle arts of persuasion and seduction.

Sound Effects	The noises made by things and events which are not easily reproduced in the studio. They are taken from specialist CDs or specially recorded in advance.
Speakers	The loudspeakers in the control room through which performances can be heard while being either recorded or replayed.
Spill	Unwanted sound being picked up by a live microphone. Sometimes coming from headphones and sometimes from an adjoining studio.
Splice	Joining two pieces of recording tape together or joining two areas of digitally recorded sound together in a computer.
Spokesman	A person who makes a commercial by speaking on behalf of a company rather than pretending to be part of it.
Spot FX	Sound effects which can easily be produced in the studio.
Staccato	A delivery which is short and sharp but not fast.
Stand-By	The traditional early warning of an impending recording.
Station Ident	The way a radio or TV station identifies itself on-air.
Statutory Words	Disclaimers or explanations which have to accompany commercials offering credit, loans, or investment opportunities.
Stereo	Two loudspeakers each relaying a slightly different version of a sound to trick the brain into creating a sense of depth and position.
Stereo Picture	The exact position in which sounds are 'placed'. Left, right, close, distant, or any combination thereof.
Studio Manager	The BBC name for a recording engineer.
Synchronising	Causing two or more events or recordings to happen simultaneously, or making two recording devices start, stop, and run together.
Tag	The last line of a commercial – often intended to be catchy or memorable.
Tagman	A person specialising in the performing of tags.
Tail	The spoken end of a commercial or the physical end of reel of recorded tape.
Tail Out	To come to a messy end – often by improvising. Also a way of storing recorded magnetic tape so that it needs to be rewound before being played. It causes any print through to occur as a more acceptable post-echo and not as an unacceptable pre-echo.

Take	One of a series of recordings of the same thing or, if you're a 'one take wonder', the only one!
Talent	American term for a male or female voice-over artist. 'Who's the talent today?'
Talkback	The system by which the engineer protects you from hearing what is being said about you in the control room. You can only hear when he chooses to press the talkback button, thereby routing the talkback mic to your cans. Your mic is live – they can always hear what you say about them, so don't!
Tape	An old-fashioned medium for recording and transmitting sound. Sometimes still used in emergencies.
Tape Op	Employed to operate the tape recorders, make tea, and generally take the blame. Pecks slightly higher than a runner.
Timeline	A piece of software capable of making a 32-second performance fit a 29-second commercial. Not much used the other way round.
Top	The beginning of a script or recording. Also known as the 'front'.
Track	Can refer to the whole recording or one separate element within it, such as the voice, music, or effects.
Track Ident	Same as 'slate' or 'ident'.
Trailer	A broadcast advertisement for something soon to be broadcast on either the same or a related station. In the USA this is the name given to the cinema film which advertises a forthcoming feature.
Trails	The BBC department which produces trailers.
Turn	The technique of putting subtle pitch changes within a word to make it more interesting or to change its meaning.
Two Hander	A commercial script which involves interaction between two or more people – whether or not they ever meet each other.
Type Casting	The system which now dominates the world of voice-overs and commercials and which has further reduced the employment opportunities for people who can act.
V/O	Script shorthand for voice-over.
Visuals	In television commercial scripts the written description of what will be seen.
Vocal Age	The perceived age of a voice rather than the actual age of its perpetrator.
Voice Agency	A theatrical agent specialising in representing voices and who's books are full unless

	you happen to be famous or incredibly persistent!
Voice Prompt	Machines which have been trained to answer the telephone and, by pretending to be human, trick you into playing all sorts of silly games involving numbers, hashes and stars. When they tire of this they connect you to a real person – so that you can shout at them about how much time you've just wasted.
Warrington Minge	A fictitious character believed to have been created by the late Peter Sellers. He was a very 'plummy' English 'Actor-Laddie' and featured in a famous story in which he unsuccessfully attempted to get a cheque cashed. His name has passed into English voice-over folklore and is used to describe a very comical old-fashioned style of delivery. The mere mention of his name can reduce actors and musicians to tears of laughter and someone will always quote the famous punchline to the story 'In that case, dear boy, could you iron the bloody thing for me?'
Word/Time Ratio	The number of words to be delivered in a given time. It is very seldom that client and voice-over agree about this.
Wrap	That's it, finished, the end.

13

The CD

The CD contains a performance of each of the commercial and narration scripts. Where two performers' names are credited, the first is for the British CD and the second is for the version available in the USA. Each track also contains the jingle, music, and/or special effects used (without the voice) so that you can try the script yourself. Scripts that require you to start at the same time as the music begin with the reverse count.

There are examples of good and bad microphone technique, and the effect of different processors on a speaking voice.

1. A delightful evening **Gillie Gratham or Dian Perry**
2. A disastrous evening **Lisette Mitchiner**
3. Bombay Sapphire **Angela McHale or Sergio Marini**
4. Viking Direct **Michael Mears or Dian Perry**
5. Pantene Hair Spray **Angela McHale or Dian Perry**
6. MAK Car Care Centres **Gillie Gratham or Dian Perry**
7. BT Callminder **Michael Mears**
8. English Breakfast Tea **Michael Mears or Ken Oxtoby**
9. Crisis **Kevin Quarmby**
10. Black Gold **Laura Bazeley or Dian Perry**
11. Sky Digital **Caroline Shaw (child) with Ken Oxtoby or Dian Perry**
12. Summit Furniture **James Weber Brown**
13. Hoseasons Holidays **Sue Holness**
14. Rap and Hard-core Collection **Hazel Holder or Sergio Marini**
15. Hargreaves of Taunton **Ken Oxtoby**
16. Invicta Motors **Brian Hales**
17. Black Magic Chocolates **Ken Oxtoby or Dian Perry**
18. Birds of the Seashore **James Weber Brown**
19. Tanker Safety **Ken Oxtoby or Sergio Marini**
20. Vitiligo **Hazel Holder**
21. Thin Walled Tube **Ken Oxtoby**
22. Quinta Da Rosa **Gillie Gratham or Dian Perry**
23. Leeds Castle **Janine Cooper or Dian Perry**
24. Computer Skills **Jacqui Compton**

25. The Big Banger **Brian Hales**
26. Intergalactic Federation **Sergio Marini**
27. Continuity Script **Gillie Gratham**
28. Sports Trailer **Sergio Marini**
29. Voice Prompt System **Jacqui Compton or Dian Perry**
30. The Dragon Who Couldn't Help Breathing Fire **Katie Corrie**
31. Wine Bar Atmos
32. Speaking at the standard distance from the mic
33. Speaking very close to the mic demonstrating the proximity effect
34. Popping! A demonstration of over-projection
35. A voice not being compressed
36. A voice being compressed
37. A voice being over compressed with breaths being accentuated
38. A voice being harmonised up
39. A voice being harmonised down
40. A voice with added echo
41. A voice with added reverb
42. A useful reverse count

14

Useful Contacts, Books, Websites

WEBSITES

If you put 'voice-overs' into a search engine you usually get 500,000 sites to look at! The following will link you into the world of voice-overs on the internet.

www.bernardshaw.co.uk
I wrote this book – this is my site through which I can be contacted. The voice-overs on the CD can be contacted through me.

www.sound.co.uk
The best voice-over site I have ever come across. Contains an astonishing amount of very useful information and advice. The are many links to other sites. This is where you can find accurate information about voice-over fees in the UK.

www.toonvoices.com
The best USA site I have ever seen. It contains a wealth of information and many useful links to other sites. This is where you can find out about voice-over fees in the USA.

www.excellentvoice.co.uk
An excellent site containing much useful information and advice. It gives you the chance to hear the showreels of some very successful voice-overs. Have a look at their 'Frequently Asked Questions'

pages – and then sent them a tape, if you dare!

www.voiceovers.co.uk
A site where experienced voice-overs, and newcomers, can advertise themselves. Contains interesting information and useful contacts.

www.rhubarb.com
A fun and complex site from one of London's very successful agencies.

www.hobsons-international.com
Another of the top London agencies.

www.spokenword.com
The site for USA 'talent' Beau Weaver. The site contains good advice for people wanting to work in voice-overs. Mr Weaver is regarded as one of the very best practitioners of the art of self-promotion.

www.radiotvschool.co.uk
The training school for radio presenters – a very interesting site.

www.bbc.co.uk
One of the best and most visited sites in the world. Contains a huge amount of information and access to scripts and programme transcripts. There are job advertisements!

www.radioacademy.org
If you're in radio in the UK then you are in The Radio Academy.

This is the site for radio professionals and contains invaluable information and links.
www.irdp.co.uk
This is the definitive site for radio acting. Contains complete scripts and extracts from productions. Many excellent worldwide links and a wealth of information.
www.ukc.ac.uk
A very interesting site with much to interest radio academics.
www.thestage.co.uk
This is the place where voice-over jobs are advertised. The site is updated every Thursday morning. Contains news, information, and links.
www.spotlightcd.com
The Spotlight publish the *UK Directory of Actors and Actresses* and a number of other useful books. They also have a free career advisory service which can be contacted on 020 7437 7631. They might be able to tell you which voice agents are taking on new clients and they will certainly be able to tell you where to get a voice tape made.

SUPPLIERS

Mo Dutta Organisation, 1b Calthorpe Mansions Birmingham B15 1QS. Tel: 0121 248 0200. *www.modutta.com* Suppliers of ISYS Pro – the PC-based codec which has simplified ISDN connections.
Studiospares, 61–63 Rochester Place, London, NW1 9JU. Tel: 020 7482 1692.
www.studiospares.com are the leading suppliers of studio equipment and consumables. This is where to get professional cassettes and labels.
Viking Direct, PO Box 187,

Leicester LE4 1ZZ. Tel: 0800 42 44 44. *www.viking-direct.co.uk* supply office equipment. Their padded envelopes (used for sending out tapes and CDs) are exceptionally good value. They also sell labels and labelling software for cassettes and CDs.

BOOKS

Voice-Over Contacts 2000. This is the only UK book specialising in voice-over contacts. It is invaluable: £15.95 inc. post and packing only from Osborne Production, Osborne House, 221 Moselle Avenue, London N22 6EY. Tel: 020 8881 0692. *Broadcast Production Guide* – an Emap Business Publication. c. £70.00. This lists all the production companies and allied trades in the UK. Voice-overs can have their details included free of charge.

The following books are all relatively inexpensive and are available from *www.amazon.co.uk* or *www.amazon.com*
Radio Acting by Alan Beck (A & C Black)
Acting Strangely by Martin Jarvis (Methuen)
About Acting by Peter Barkworth (Methuen)
For All Occasions by Peter Barkworth (Methuen)
Make Acting Work by Chrys Salt (Bloomsbury Publishing)
Contacts published by The Spotlight
Actor's Audition Speeches by Jean Marlow (A & C Black, London; Heinemann, New Hampshire)
Actresses' Audition Speeches by Jean Marlow (A & C Black,

London; Heinemann, New
Hampshire)
*Classical Audition Speeches for
Women* by Jean Marlow
(A & C Black, London; Heine-
mann, New Hampshire)
*Classical Audition Speeches for
Men* by Jean Marlow
(A & C Black, London; Heine-
mann, New Hampshire)
Writing for Radio by Rosemary
Horstmann (A & C Black,
London; Heinemann, New
Hampshire) contains a useful list
of published radio scripts.
*The Right to Speak: Working
with the Voice* by Patsy Rosen-
burg (Methuen, London;
Routledge/Theatre Arts, New
York).
The Voice Book by Michael
McCallion (Faber & Faber,
London; Routledge/Theatre Arts,
New York).
Voice and Speech in the Theatre
by J. Clifford Turner (A & C
Black, London; Routledge/Theatre
Arts, New York).

COURSES

The City Literary Institute,
Stukely Street, London, WC2B
5LJ. Tel: 020 7430 0544. Offers
many first class short courses in
radio acting and voice work.
The University of Kent, Canter-
bury, CT2 7NK. Tel: 01227
764000.

Alan Beck, author of *Radio
Acting*, runs the excellent and
unique Radio Drama Course.
A.E.B.Beck@ukc.ac.uk
The Actors Centre, 1a Tower St,
London, WC2H 9NP.
Tel: 020 7240 3940. Offers
occasional voice-over courses and
classes.
The Radio & TV School,
7–9 The Broadway, Newbury,
Berks, Tel: 01635 232800.
Runs training courses for radio
presenters.
Goldsmiths College, University of
London, New Cross, London,
SE14 6NW. Tel: 020 7919 7171.
Offers many full- and part-time
courses in acting and radio and
television production.

ISDN FACILITIES

A1 Vox, 20 Old Compton Street,
London W1D 4TW. Tel: 020
7434 4404; Fax: 020 7434 4414.
www.a1vox.com
A1 Vox are a central London
voice studio with a self-operated
ISDN facility available to hire for
multiples of 15 minute sessions.
You can either pay a straight hire
fee or a percentage of the money
earned whilst using it. They also
have a larger ISDN studio which
is not self-op. They are pioneering
the system of 'resident voices' –
voice artists go there every day
and wait for work to come in.

Index